DEPOSITION RULES

THE POCKET GUIDE TO WHO, WHAT, WHEN, WHERE, WHY, AND HOW

SIXTH EDITION

D0144173

NATIONAL INSTITUTE FOR TRIAL ADVOCACY

DEPOSITION RULES

THE POCKET GUIDE TO WHO, WHAT, WHEN, WHERE, WHY, AND HOW

SIXTH EDITION

David M. Malone

Ryan M. Malone

Ropes & Gray LLP
Washington, DC

Address inquiries to:

Reprint Permission
National Institute for Trial Advocacy
1685 38th Street, Suite 200
Boulder, CO 80301-2735
Phone: (800) 225-6482
Fax: (720) 890-7069
E-mail: permissions@nita.org

ISBN 978-1-60156-496-2 (print)
eISBN 978-1-60156-508-2 (ebook)
FBA 1496

Library of Congress Cataloging-in-Publication Data

Malone, David M., 1944- author.
    Deposition rules : the pocket guide to who, what, when, where, why,
    and how / David M. Malone, Ryan M. Malone. — Sixth Edition.
        pages cm
    ISBN 978-1-60156-496-2
        1. Depositions—United States. I. Malone, Ryan, 1977- author.
        II. Title.
    KF8900.M338 2015
    347.73'72—dc23

                                                              2015013626

Printed in the United States.

Contents

Introduction xv

Chapter One—Who

1.1 Who Can Be Deposed? 1

1.2 Who May Ask Questions at Depositions? 3

1.3 Can Witnesses and Nonwitnesses Both Be Deposed? 5

1.4 Can Organizations Be Deposed? 5

1.5 How Many People Can Be Deposed? 11

1.6 Can Testifying Experts Be Deposed? 12

1.7 Can Nontestifying Experts Be Deposed? 14

1.8 Who Pays Expert Fees for Depositions? ... 17

1.9 Can Senior Officials Be Deposed? 20

1.10 Can Insiders or Outsiders to the Litigation Be Excluded from the Deposition Room, and May Future Deponents Be Excluded? 21

1.11 Who Takes Custody of the Transcript? 25

Contents

Chapter Two—What

2.1 What May Be Asked?............................ 27

2.2 What Questions May the Attorney
     Direct the Witness Not to Answer? 28

2.3 What Is the Significance of an
     "Irrelevance Objection"?...................... 31

2.4 What Should Be Done about
     Coaching? 31

2.5 What May You Ask the Deponent to
     Speculate or Guess About? 33

2.6 What May You Ask about the Contents
     of Documents? 35

2.7 What Application Does the "Best
     Evidence Rule" Have at Depositions? 36

2.8 What Use May Be Made of Prior
     Statements by the Deponent?............. 40

2.9 What Reference May Be Made to
     Testimony by Other Witnesses?.......... 41

2.10 What Protection Is Provided to Secrets
     or Confidences?................................... 42

2.11 What Protection Is Provided for
     Attorney Work Product?...................... 45

2.12 What Problems Should Be Corrected
     at the Time of the Deposition?........... 48

2.13 What Can Be Asked about the Expert's Opinion in this Case?........................ 52

2.14 What Can Be Asked about the Expert's Opinions in Other Cases? 54

2.15 What Are the "Usual Stipulations"?....... 58

2.16 What Questions Must the Witness Answer Despite Objection? 60

2.17 What Must Be Supplemented in an Expert's Deposition?.......................... 60

2.18 What Must Be Supplemented in a Nonexpert's Deposition? 62

2.19 What Corrections May Be Made to the Deposition (and When May They Be Made)? 63

2.20 What Are Legitimate Bases for Objection?.. 67

2.21 What Sanctions Apply for Failure to Make Discovery at Depositions?......... 72

Chapter Three—When

3.1 May Depositions Be Taken before the Complaint Is Filed? 75

3.2 May Depositions Be Taken Pending Appeal?... 76

3.3   When, after the Discovery Conference, May Depositions Begin?...................... 77

3.4   When May Testifying Experts Be Deposed?.. 79

3.5   When May You Get Some Priority for Depositions?.. 83

3.6   When Should Depositions and Returns on Requests for Production of Documents Be Scheduled? 85

3.7   When May Formal Corrections Be Made to the Deposition?.................... 86

3.8   When May You Take a Break?............. 88

3.9   When Do Depositions Begin and End?.. 91

Chapter Four—Where

4.1   Where Must Depositions Be Taken?...... 95

4.2   Where May Party Witnesses Be Deposed?.. 96

4.3   In the Forum, at Whose Office Is a Deposition Held? 97

4.4   Where Does Everybody Sit? 98

4.5   Where Do Subpoenas Issue From? 99

4.6	Where Do Protective Orders Issue From?................................ 100
4.7	Where Do Orders to Terminate or Resume Issue From? 100
4.8	Where Are the Notary and Reporter in a Telephone Deposition? 101
4.9	Where Do the Documents Go When the Deposition Is Finished? 101

Chapter Five—Why

5.1	Why Take Depositions of Your Own Witnesses? 105
5.2	Why Should You Use Depositions to Support Motions Practice? 107
5.3	Why Do Depositions Help Uncover New Information Better than Interrogatories?................................... 109
5.4	Why Do Depositions Help Confirm Known Information?........................ 110
5.5	Why Are Depositions Useful to Support Settlement Discussions?...... 111
5.6	Why Are Interrogatories and Requests for Admission Inferior to Depositions?..................................... 112

Contents

5.7 Why Should Counsel Taking the Deposition Avoid Arguing with Defending Counsel? 113

Chapter Six—How

6.1 How Do You Notify the Witness to Appear? 117

6.2 How Do You Obtain Protection from Unreasonable Timing? 118

6.3 How Do You Protect Your Client from Improper Process? 119

6.4 How Do You Start the Deposition? 119

6.5 How Should You Frame Questions to Obtain New Information Efficiently? 121

6.6 How Do You Use Leading Questions Effectively? 121

6.7 How Can You Repeat Questions to Obtain Refined Answers? 122

6.8 How Should Deposing Counsel Control the Pace of the Deposition? 124

6.9 How to Object to Opponent's Behavior? 125

6.10 How Do You Make Designations of Transcript that You May Use at Trial? 127

6.11 How Does Your Client Communicate with You during the Deposition?...... 128

6.12 How Do You Handle Exhibits at Deposition?...................................... 129

6.13 How Do You Number Exhibits at Deposition?...................................... 131

Chapter Seven—Expert Depositions

7.1 What Is the Relationship between the Expert Report and the Expert Deposition?.................................... 133

7.2 What Is the Most Important Question to Ask at an Expert's Deposition?...................................... 136

7.3 What Is the Most Important Preparation for the Expert's Deposition?...................................... 137

7.4 What Is the "Fourteen Document Rule," and How Do You Use It to Prepare Your Expert? 138

Contents

7.5   How Protective Should You Be of the Expert at the Deposition?................. 139

7.6   What Role Does Your Expert Have in the Deposition of the Opposing Expert?... 140

7.7   What Is the Relationship between *Daubert* and the Expert's Deposition?...................................... 141

The *Daubert* Deposition Dance: Retracing the Intricacies of the Expert's Steps...................................... 145

Chapter Eight—Video Depositions

8.1   Why Should You Take a Video Deposition?...................................... 171

8.2   How Do You Adjust Your Defense in a Video Deposition?..................... 173

8.3   How Do You Obtain Rulings on Objections to Material in a Video Deposition?...................................... 175

8.4   When Do You Need a Paper or Computer Transcript of a Video Deposition?...................................... 176

8.5   How Do You Use a Video Deposition
      at Trial? 176

8.6   When Should You Use the Video
      Deposition at Trial? 180

Chapter Nine—Seven Ways to Use Depositions at Trial

9.1   Testimony of an Absent Witness. 183

9.2   Past Recollection Recorded. 184

9.3   Basis for Proffer. 185

9.4   Refreshing Recollection. 185

9.5   Source of Opposing Party Statement
      (or Admission). 186

9.6   Impeachment. 187

9.7   Phantom Impeachment. 188

INTRODUCTION

This guide provides a quick reference to the rules, procedures, and practices that govern deposition practice, and it attempts to answer the most commonly asked questions about depositions. The federal rules are used as the basic framework for deposition practice. Rule references are to the Federal Rules of Civil Procedure as amended December 1, 2014, unless otherwise indicated. Where important, situations in which state or local practice may differ are discussed. The informal style of this book is intended to provide accessible, practical, easily understandable advice. Most users may want to start by looking for their topic of interest in the index or table of contents to find the quickest path to the relevant text.

The "Practice Tips" are drawn from the actual conduct of counsel in depositions, because modern deposition practice has evolved at least as much from "what works" as it has from "what is required."

Introduction

The discussion in this handbook of the rules and practice affecting depositions has been kept brief, emphasizing identification, but not complete explanation, of issues to facilitate its use as a ready and convenient, on-the-go reference. For more extended discussion of any matters presented here, refer to *The Effective Deposition: Techniques and Strategies That Work*, by David M. Malone and Peter T. Hoffman (NITA).

CHAPTER ONE

WHO

1.1 Who Can Be Deposed?

A deposition may be taken of any person or organization who is within the jurisdiction of a federal court (FED. R. CIV. P. 30(a)). For parties and persons controlled by a party—officers, directors, managing agents, 30(b)(6) designees, and such—a "notice" of deposition is sent to the party's counsel, and that notice is sufficient to compel attendance; for others, like nonparties or low-level employees of a party, a Rule 45 subpoena is required. The court compelling attendance is the forum court, when the deponent is a party or is located within the forum district, or the district court for the district where the deposition is to take place (FED. R. CIV. P. 45(a)(2)).

_____

Practice Comment

When deciding whether or not a deposition is permitted, remember to start from the premise that "discovery is allowed unless it is forbidden." Therefore, unless there is some rule or protective order stating that a particular category of witness cannot be deposed (e.g., nontestifying experts (FED. R. CIV. P. 26(b)(4)(D)), those persons are subject to deposition. (Depositions of foreign persons on foreign soil involve U.S. treaty obligations, not mere subpoena power, and they are beyond the scope of this book.) A more interesting question is whether a witness *should* be deposed, given that the opposing party is entitled to attend depositions. If the potential witness is not an employee, representative, or officer of the opposing party, he can probably be interviewed without the opposing party or its counsel present. Thus, just as the opposing party can speak with employees and others without telling you about it, so you can talk to some potential witnesses without telling the opposing party. If the testimony turns out not to be helpful, you would not have to disclose your conversation. If the conversation turns out to be helpful, you can list them as witnesses, depose them yourself if there is a question about their availability for trial, or attend the other side's deposition of them, with you participating not as counsel to the witness, but as attorney for your client. (We are not discussing here the *Jencks*- or *Brady*-type obligations to reveal witness statements that many federal government agencies have taken on themselves in civil cases. Those are a matter more of internal policies than of legal obligations.)

1.2 Who May Ask Questions at Depositions?

Federal Rule of Civil Procedure 29, by its breadth, suggests that the parties may stipulate that anyone may ask questions at a deposition. In antitrust and similarly complex matters, counsel have sometimes agreed that forensic economists and accountants may ask questions, especially of deponents who themselves are forensic economists or accountants. This practice is not recommended, because of the significant possibility that the experts will quickly come to speak with one another in the jargon of their trade, not only creating an opaque record, but confusing the attorneys and others who have a right to participate. Furthermore, regardless of any stipulations by the parties' counsel, there are states that treat questioning and defending at depositions as "the practice of law," which would logically mean that those nonlawyer questioners would be engaged in the practice of law without a license. (Other states require the "unlicensed lawyer" to be representing someone before a "tribunal" of some sort before there is a violation of the rules regarding unauthorized practice.) Whether the deposition questioning would subject a nonlawyer to possible penalties for unauthorized practice is a legal question that the expert or other questioner may need advice on. Who pays for such advice, whether this is truly a service to the actual client, and whether the expert is then the client of the main client's lawyer—these are questions that may persuade any lawyer that the fight is not worth it. Trial counsel has better things to do. In addition, the lawyer is the one who has received training in questioning and in deposition procedures.

1.3 Can Witnesses and Nonwitnesses Both Be Deposed?

Witnesses and nonwitnesses may both be deposed. The deponent need not even be a witness or potential witness (FED. R. CIV. P. 26(b)(1)). The deponent could be a person who is known not to be a witness, but who may have information leading to the identification of potential witnesses, documents, or other relevant evidence. For example, the shipping dock supervisor may be deposed to find out who had access to certain records or shipments, and then those workers might become witnesses while the supervisor happily stays away.

1.4 Can Organizations Be Deposed?

An organization (corporation, partnership, association, government agency, etc.) may be called to be deposed by a party; the organization must then designate a person or persons who will testify about matters known or reasonably available to the organization (FED. R. CIV. P. 30(b)(6)). The notice of deposition to an organization that is a party or the subpoena to an organization that is not a party must specify the time, date, and place of the deposition, but does not specify the person to be deposed; instead, it appends "specifications" or a list of topics on which the deposition is to be held, exactly analogous to the specifications in a request for production of documents. In modern practice in most federal courts today, this list does not restrict the questioner, but only notifies the deponent that at least these topics may be raised. Best practice is that the topics beyond the list of specifications do not give rise to admissions. The organization, party or nonparty, then chooses its designated speaker—the designee or designees—and prepares them for the deposition by providing them with information reasonably within the organization's reach and responsive to the specifications. Where the deponent is a party, the answers to questions within the specifications constitute an opposing party's statement (FED. R. EVID. 801(d)(2)(C)) and are binding unless a court allows contradicting evidence. The designees may be questioned on topics outside the specifications, but their answers are then not considered to be answers by the party and are therefore an opposing party's statement. Answers from designees named by nonparties are obviously not an opposing party's statement, whether the questions were within or without the topics on the list of specifications.

Practice Comment

Remember that the person designated by the organization is speaking on behalf of the organization when he is answering in topic areas from the specifications—therefore, regardless of whether the witness is an officer, director, managing agent, or other designee of a party, the deposition testimony constitutes an opposing party's statement under Federal Rule of Evidence 801(d)(2). In fact, Federal Rule of Civil Procedure 32(a)(3) specifically recognizes this effect by stating "[a]n adverse party may use for any purpose the deposition of . . . the party's . . . designee under Rule 30(b)(b). . . ." Furthermore, if multiple designees are provided, the questioner should ask each to identify the specifications he will address to make certain that no specifications are overlooked. With multiple designees, each may be deposed for the full seven-hour day, although the entire response is considered to be one deposition of the organization.

Where the target of a Rule 30(b)(6) deposition is a nonparty, counsel taking the deposition must advise the nonparty organization, in the subpoena, of its obligations to designate deponents to respond on behalf of the organization. In addition, although this is not explicitly stated in the rule, counsel should advise the nonparty of its obligation to conduct a reasonable search for information to be provided by the designees, if they do not already possess it.

There is a tactical reason for using Rule 30(b)(6) where the information sought might be contained in historic records of the organization: an interrogatory seeking the same information is often properly met with the argument that the information is equally available to both parties from the documents and that the burden of searching through those documents should rest on the party seeking the information, as the rules allow (FED. R. CIV. P. 33(d)). Rule 30(b)(6) depositions, however, do not allow such "burden shifting," and the target of the deposition notice or subpoena must conduct a reasonable inquiry to obtain the information identified in the specifications. At the deposition, the 30(b)(6) deponent may only correctly answer "I don't know" when the organization, having conducted a reasonable inquiry for the information, was unable to obtain it. The fact that the deponent lacks personal knowledge will not support such an answer, since he is testifying not as himself, but as the organization, and the designee is charged with the organization's knowledge if it can be reasonably determined.

A final note about Rule 30(b)(6) depositions:

When selecting a designee, an organization is advised not to get too cute. One Minneapolis hospital corporation chose its general counsel as the designee, who then proceeded to claim attorney-client privilege in response to most deposition questions, since everything he knew he had learned from his client. When the opposing party protested that he was an improper designee, the court disagreed, saying that the hospital was entitled to choose its designee; but, by choosing the general counsel, the hospital had waived all attorney-client privilege. The deposition was ordered to proceed. This case is extreme, and choosing an attorney may have waiver consequences if the lawyer does not claim privilege or get into parts of privileged communications or work product. Nevertheless, it is an area in which to be careful. A recently retired executive, with some knowledge of the business surrounding the dispute, but no knowledge as a direct participant, is probably the best designee.

1.5 How Many People Can Be Deposed?

Rule 30(a)(2)(A) allows ten depositions per party without leave of court; local rules often reduce this number. Where leave of court is obtained, of course, the number is limited only by time, expense, and other practical concerns. Multiple Rule 30(b)(6) designees responding to a single notice or subpoena count as only one deposition—that of the organization that designated them. Of course, if the designee is also deposed as a named defendant, that would count as an additional deposition.

Practice Comment

Many federal district and state courts have adopted their own limitations on the number of depositions. Counsel should check the local rules as well as the judge's own rules for limitations. Such limitations are often phrased in terms of a limit on nonparty depositions, to allow an adequate number of party depositions where there are multiple plaintiffs or defendants and in third-party practice.

1.6 Can Testifying Experts Be Deposed?

Depositions of testifying experts are allowed (FED. R. CIV. P. 26(b)(4)).

Practice Comment

The depositions of testifying experts have become much more important in these last twenty years or so, principally because of the exponential increase in the use of experts in litigation, and also because of the 1993 Supreme Court decision in *Daubert*, which, together with *Kumho Tire*, required that expert testimony be founded on reliable methodologies as shown to the court by reasonably competent evidence. The "*Daubert* reliability" issue has become a major focus of pretrial discovery and motions practice. Indeed, the trial court's dismissal of the *Kumho Tire* case was based solely on the deposition testimony of the plaintiff's expert on tire failure, which persuaded the Supreme Court that the expert for the plaintiffs had misapplied the methodology he said that he was using. The expert's testimony was stricken, and the case was dismissed, without remand. As more civil cases present complex expert testimony, it obviously becomes more important to examine the opponent's expert testimony for flaws at deposition. Pretrial challenges are common, with or without "*Daubert* hearings" under Federal Rule of Evidence 104 out of the hearing of the jury, and the information for cross-examination at those hearings and for argument in those motions is normally obtained in deposition, based in part on the expert's report. It is standard to take these depositions at the end of discovery, and the rules require that they be taken after the expert's report is received

(FED. R. CIV. P. 26(b)(4)(A)). Despite the hopes of the Advisory Committee, the mandatory expert reports do not seem to have shortened expert depositions; as most experienced litigators would guess, more paper raises more questions. Expert reports instead have probably lengthened expert depositions—counsel ask not only about the report, but then conduct a complete deposition on the standard topics. Stipulations at the Federal Rule of Civil Procedure 26(f) conference should cover the extension of expert depositions (or any other witness's deposition, for that matter) beyond the allotted day, if the parties anticipate such a need.

1.7 Can Nontestifying Experts Be Deposed?

Nontestifying experts may not be deposed and need not be identified, absent court order (FED. R. CIV. P. 26(b)(4)(D)). The rationale behind the consulting witness is that attorneys may need help deciding whether a testifying expert is needed as well as what the testifying expert himself needs, is doing, or is saying. The consulting expert can be a link between the science and the attorney; the consulting expert is not intended to be a link between the attorney, the case, and the testifying expert. Therefore, the consulting expert, like attorneys and paralegals on the case, supports the attorney team and enjoys work-product and other protections under this rule. The 2010 amendments to Rule 26 protect, as privileged attorney work product, communications between the attorney and the testifying expert as long as they do not convey facts or data considered by the expert; assumptions relied on by the expert; or fee arrangements with the expert. In some instances—for example, where a government employee leaves the government and becomes a consultant in the private sector—he may retain knowledge making him valuable as a consulting witness, but at the same time possess factual knowledge of the working of the government machinery. In such a case, he may be deposed as a fact witness while remaining unavailable for deposition as a consulting witness because of this rule's protections.

Practice Comment

Be careful not to misuse the nontestifying or consulting witness as a conduit for information you want the testifying expert to have. The testifying expert can be asked about facts or assumptions that he has "considered" (a logical extension from the use of "considered" in describing what subjects must be contained in the expert report), even if they came from the attorney. He will probably also have to discuss what he has learned from the consulting expert, and he may have to identify the consulting expert so that the testifying expert's decision to use the obtained information can be scrutinized for reasonableness. However, because the opposing party can learn what the testifying expert considered without going to the consulting expert, even such heavy reliance may not expose the consulting expert to direct discovery. The expert who is a consultant to the attorney is to be distinguished from the people (even other experts) who are subordinate to the testifying expert (in his firm or group, for example); those subordinates may supply information directly to the testifying expert, of course, but they are also quite routinely subjected to deposition. They are not consulting experts—they are sources to, or extensions of, the testifying expert herself. Imagine a fence between the attorney and the testifying expert: the consulting expert stands with the attorney on one side; the juniors and assistants to the testifying expert stand with him on the other side.

1.8 Who Pays Expert Fees for Depositions?

The party obtaining deposition discovery from a testifying expert must pay the expert's reasonable fees that result from attending and participating in the deposition (FED. R. CIV. P. 26(b)(4)(E)).

In the "exceptional circumstances" where non-testifying experts are allowed to be deposed, they are entitled to both reasonable fees and expenses (FED. R. CIV. P. 26(b)(4)(E)). As a practical matter, testifying experts are routinely reimbursed for their expenses by the deposing party for providing deposition testimony. Those fees and expenses are routinely included in costs, when costs are allocated at the end of the litigation.

Practice Comment

Opposing counsel often agree, in advance, that each will bear the costs and associated expenses of their own experts' attendance and participation at depositions. Because counsel or the client employing the expert already has a contractual relationship with the expert, this practice makes sense. Any stipulation to this effect, however, should note that the parties retain the right to apply to the court for protection, either in the form of a limiting order or in the form of an order requiring reimbursement of fees or expenses if the deposition process is abused.

Such an order is specifically authorized by Rule 26(c). This agreement between counsel is logical, because an attorney does not want his expert unhappy with the trial process because opposing counsel has delayed or challenged the payment of fees and expenses. Even where there is no agreement, it would make sense for sponsoring counsel (and the client) to pay his expert witness's fees and to then seek reimbursement under this rule from the opposing party who took the deposition. In the unusual case where substantial deposition time is used by the sponsoring attorney, perhaps to create a preservation transcript to be used if the expert is absent from trial or to create a record of responses to *Daubert* challenges to use at a hearing, counsel who noticed the discovery deposition could of course seek repayment of a proportional share of the costs of the deposition—expert fees and expenses included. The time that an expert spends with counsel or on his own preparing to give his deposition is not a chargeable cost and is not included in the expenses and fees payable by the deposing party.

1.9 Can Senior Officials Be Deposed?

Senior officials of parties—like the chief executive officer, chairman of the board, or chief operating or financial officer—may be deposed, although some protection is available to prevent abuse and disruption of business activities. Some courts have ruled that if a protective order is sought by the company and it shows that the executives do not have unique factual information about the matter giving rise to the lawsuit (as, for example, was the case with regard to a wrongful death by auto where depositions were sought of the topmost executives of a car company who were not personally involved in the design, manufacture, or retail sale of the automobile that crashed), their depositions would not be permitted until other, less intrusive discovery was attempted. *See Alberto v. Toyota Motor Corp.*, 2010 WL 3057755 (Mich. Ct. App. Aug. 5, 2010), for a decision and dissent reviewing the history and availability of such protection in the government and private context. This is known as the "apex-deposition" rule, and it was originally created to prevent disruption at high levels of government.

Practice Comment

Abuse of participants in litigation, parties and nonparties alike, is inappropriate and violates a number of duties that the profession owes to the public. Just as a practical matter, if you abuse your opponent's senior people, you have little right to expect gentle treatment of your senior people. Such actions have no place in modern discovery, and no client is entitled to any advantage gained by such misbehavior.

1.10 Can Insiders or Outsiders to the Litigation Be Excluded from the Deposition Room, and May Future Deponents Be Excluded?

Insiders—that is, the parties and their agents, the deponent, counsel, the officer administering the

oath, and the court reporter and videographer—
are entitled to be present at a deposition and
cannot be removed without a stipulation or order,
regardless of the location of the deposition (that
is, no matter which counsel hosts the proceeding).
Outsiders—including members of the public,
other witnesses, relatives of witnesses, members of
the media, and counsel not of record in the instant
case-are not excluded by any rule, but may be
excluded by a protective order issued by the court
(FED. R. CIV. P. 26(c)(1)(E)).

Practice Comment

According to the language of the rules,
depositions are not closed proceedings;
they are instead part of the public
disposition of civil litigation, of which
the trial is also a part. Nevertheless,
many counsel and judges continue
to believe that depositions are private
and that "outsiders" may be excluded as a
matter of right. The existence of Rule 26(c)
(1)(E) should have concluded discussion
on this question long ago, because there

would be little sense in recognizing the specific authority of the court to limit those who may attend a deposition if depositions were normally closed proceedings. As a practical matter, because most depositions take place in private conference rooms, people not formally associated with the case can be excluded by the host party or counsel controlling the room through tenancy or ownership. The visiting party, however, has no such right and would have to apply to the court to exclude people unless home-court counsel agrees to treat the intruding people as trespassers.

A related question that often arises is whether future deponents may attend depositions. In Rule 30(c), which provides that examination and cross-examination will "proceed as they would at trial," the language "except Rules 103 and 615" has been included. Rule 615 is the "rule on witnesses," providing that at the request of any party, witnesses will be excluded from the courtroom until after they testify. By specifically excluding Rule 615 from the rules applying to depositions, the authors of the amendments to Federal Rules of Civil Procedure are recognizing that deposition witnesses may be present at depositions of other witnesses, absent a protective order.

Of course, counsel can avoid many of these problems by stipulating who may be present at the deposition. Because the method of recording the testimony can be changed by stipulation, and because the requirement of an oath can be avoided by stipulation, even the officer and the reporter are not actually necessary. Thus, at least in theory, the parties could stipulate that the witness give the deposition by speaking in a stream-of-consciousness style into a Playskool tape recorder while standing, all alone, in a broom closet. Nevertheless, it seems likely that if the public has a legitimate interest in attending, a stipulation between the parties should not be sufficient to close the deposition.

A matter for consideration is whether a party wants to object to the presence of an observer. The decision should not be knee-jerk: the presence of a reporter for *The New York Times* may put pressure on the executive who was planning to stonewall at the deposition. Therefore, the taking attorney should not be too quick to stipulate that the deposition in his own offices should be closed to outsiders-perhaps some consideration by the lawyer of the impact of publicity from the lawsuit will compel more reasonable settlement offers.

1.11 Who Takes Custody of the Transcript?

Where the deposition record is not filed with the court, the officer will send it to the attorney who requested the recording of the deposition, and that attorney will retain custody and protect the deposition record as the custodian for the court (FED. R. CIV. P. 30(f)(1)). However, by stipulation, the parties normally leave custody with the reporter; since the original is most often a computer file, the burden of maintaining custody has greatly diminished in recent years, and electronic copies of that "original" will themselves be originals under Federal Rule of Evidence 1001(3). The "original" exhibits to the depositions, themselves likely copies-but copies that have been handled and reviewed by the witness-often remain with the original transcript, but they can also be retained by counsel taking the deposition, if agreement to that procedure is reached under Federal Rule of Civil Procedure 29.

CHAPTER TWO

WHAT

2.1 What May Be Asked?

Parties may obtain discovery of any nonprivileged matter that is relevant to the issues or reasonably calculated to lead to the discovery of admissible evidence (FED. R. CIV. P. 26(b)(1)).

Practice Comment

It is important to understand that this language allows inquiry into matters that are not themselves admissible as long as they might reasonably lead to the discovery of admissible information. The best current practice allows the deposing counsel to pose questions and take answers from the deponent, regardless of defending counsel's opinions about the utility or "trial relevance" of the information being sought.

A safe rule-of-thumb is that if the material is relevant, it is presumptively discoverable; if the material reasonably leads to relevant information, it is presumptively discoverable; and the burden of showing privilege or other basis for nondiscoverability rests on the party resisting discovery.

2.2 What Questions May the Attorney Direct the Witness Not to Answer?

Instructing the witness not to answer particular questions is appropriate only where the answer would invade some recognized privilege or would exceed the permissible scope of a court order (FED. R. CIV. P. 30(c)(2)); or where the question has the effect, intentional or unintentional, of subjecting the deponent to annoyance, embarrassment, or oppression (FED. R. CIV. P. 30(d)(3)).

Practice Comment

When the deponent's counsel directs or requests the witness not to answer, the questioning attorney follows up by asking the witness whether she will answer the question, because it is the witness who has the final decision on whether to answer and who is subject to compulsion. When counsel believes that the basis for refusing to answer is inappropriate and that the matter sought to be discovered is important to further progress at the deposition, counsel might inform the witness of the consequences of her refusal—a hearing before the magistrate judge, an assignment of costs and fees, and a resumption of the deposition and spending additional time answering what should have been answered in the first place. When the witness understands the risk that she may have to pay counsel's fees, she may want some time to discuss the matter with her counsel. In any event, asking the questions again an hour later, or coming back to them again from another direction, using different language, may get the answer and make the problem moot.

On another point, it is important to remember that questioning counsel is unlikely to resolve the difference of opinion with defending counsel that leads to the direction not to answer, and such a resolution is not a realistic goal. Instead, counsel needs to discover the facts that give rise to the objection so a judge can later rule on their adequacy to prevent discovery. Therefore, if privilege is claimed as the basis for the direction not to answer, for example, questioning counsel should focus on questions that will allow the court to determine whether the privilege actually existed, has been waived, or does not apply.

2.3 What Is the Significance of an "Irrelevance Objection"?

"Lack of relevance" is not a basis for refusing discovery. There is usually no purpose in making "lack of relevance" objections at a deposition other than to attempt to provoke useless arguments between counsel. If the question is objectionable as arguably beyond the proper scope of discovery under Rule 26 or a court order because it is not reasonably calculated to lead to the production of admissible evidence, then that should be the objection. If necessary, the deposition should be halted to permit the defending party to obtain a protective order if the questioner persists in questioning that is clearly beyond the scope of Rule 26. If the deposition is not halted for this purpose, however, "beyond the scope of Rule 26" does not provide a basis for directing a witness not to answer, so the questioning—and answering—should proceed.

2.4 What Should Be Done about Coaching?

All attorneys will agree that "coaching" a witness at a deposition is improper; unfortunately, not all attorneys agree about what constitutes coaching.

In general, coaching is behavior by defending counsel that has the purpose or intent of altering the substance of the witness's testimony; it may occur before the deposition, during preparation ("If you see me just push the document aside, then you should tell them that you don't know anything about it"); at the deposition ("It ought to be clear that this witness has no information about activities before January 2014"); or in the hallway at the deposition, off the record ("Listen, when we go back in, tell them that you were mistaken, that you really don't know Mary Francis"). Regardless of where it occurs, coaching is improper. When defending counsel says, before an answer is given, "You can answer, if you know," all attorneys can recognize that as coaching, because the clear suggestion is that the witness should say that she does not know. If the same advice is given in the hallway, off the record, out of earshot, the effect is the same, but it is much harder to discover that the coaching occurred. This inappropriate behavior contrasts markedly with defending counsel who asks, "What year was that?" in place of making an "ambiguous as to time" objection. No coaching has occurred, because the attorney has not suggested substance to the witness. In fact, the record has been clarified because after the witness's answer, the time in question will be less ambiguous. However, disputes will be avoided if such clarifications are not made during the other side's questioning; they should be held for the "follow-on" examination by defending counsel.

2.5 What May You Ask the Deponent to Speculate or Guess About?

Speculation and guesswork: The witness may be requested to speculate at a deposition. Rule 26(b)(1) allows any questioning that is reasonably calculated to lead to the discovery of admissible evidence on matters not privileged.

Practice Comment

Counsel, either taking or defending depositions, often instructs the witness not to speculate. This is both inappropriate and odd. Inappropriate because there is no prohibition against obtaining a witness's speculation as long as it is "reasonably calculated to lead to the discovery of admissible evidence." For example, the crew foreman's ruminations about the cause of the ditch collapse may be speculation, but they could very well lead to further questions about the adequacy of shoring. Therefore, defending counsel may not properly instruct the witness not to speculate. Furthermore, speculation might be helpful to questioning counsel, even if it is inadmissible. Obviously, speculation by a business's chief financial officer about causes of the business's failure may be useful. Why counsel asking the questions in a discovery deposition would, against her own interests, want to caution a witness against speculation is, well, sheer speculation.

The party seeking speculation should worry about the foundation for the speculation only if the testimony turns out to be favorable. If the speculation is useful, the deposing attorney might try to lay some foundation, perhaps turning the speculation into a lay opinion under Federal Rule of Evidence 701 or into a summary of voluminous underlying data (the foreman's experience over forty years with ditches) under Rule 1006. It may be that neither approach works, but little is lost in the effort. The decision to attempt to lay foundation does not have to be made until the answer is heard and evaluated, however.

If the deponent speculates unfavorably, the deposition taker may return to the characterization of "speculation" and sympathize with the witness's discomfort about guessing, perhaps establishing that the witness has no solid foundation for the speculation, so later use by the opponent may be difficult.

2.6 What May You Ask about the Contents of Documents?

Deponents may be asked about the contents of documents and may be asked to interpret documents (FED. R. CIV. P. 26(b)). Despite folklore to the contrary, documents do not "speak for themselves" at deposition or trial. Often they need clarification and interpretation, and the deposition is the most appropriate opportunity to obtain such information. Indeed, most practitioners attempt to obtain documents before they request depositions specifically so that they can identify documentary information that needs explanation. Furthermore, a witness's understanding of a document, even if the witness was incorrect, may help explain why the witness acted as she did.

2.7 What Application Does the "Best Evidence Rule" Have at Depositions?

The availability of information in a document does not preclude inquiry into that same information at an oral deposition (FED. R. CIV. P. 26(b)). The "original document" or "best evidence rule" does not prevent a deponent from testifying about a subject that is also referenced in a document. This rule, nowadays more often called "the original document rule," merely states that when the contents of a document are sought to be proved and those contents are important to resolving an issue in the case, an original of the document should be produced or its absence satisfactorily explained. It is a combination of Rules 1002 and 1004.

Practice Comment

At a deposition, when the witness is asked about an event that also happens to be discussed in a document, the contents of the document are not sought to be proved; therefore, the "best evidence rule" does not apply. Indeed, the witness's knowledge of the event exists independently from the document and is an appropriate foundation for the testimony. Even if deposing counsel were trying to discover or "prove" the contents of a document, that testimony could be obtained at a discovery deposition because the test for discoverability is not admissibility at trial (FED. R. CIV. P. 26). Indeed, that deposition testimony about the contents may be a suitable substitute for the actual document, if the unavailability of the original document is explained (FED. R. EVID. 1002–04). There is no hierarchy among substitutes for the missing original.

Furthermore, the fact that information on a subject may be in a document, and may even have provided deposing counsel with the source of information for the question, does not mean that the questioner is limited only to what she can learn from the document. The questioner is entitled to obtain more information, or different information, or confirming information. The existence of the document is irrelevant.

Finally, because the existence of a document on a topic is irrelevant, counsel is under no obligation to disclose the document to the witness or to allow the witness to read the document before answering the question. Therefore, there is no basis for the often-heard objection: "Counsel, if you got this from some document, and I think you did, in fairness you should show it to the witness." At that point, the questioner should consider clearing the space of any documents, to emphasize the thrust of her question, and saying to the witness: "Please tell me about the meeting on widget prices that took place in December."

Once a witness is shown a document on a topic, the witness is unlikely to remember anything about that topic other than what is within the four corners of the document. The witness is perhaps hoping that is all the questioner knows, and she will refrain from venturing beyond it. Therefore, the most productive discovery strategy proceeds from open questions ("How were prices set?") to narrower questions ("Were there ever any meetings with competitors about prices?") to the narrowest questions, including document-based questions ("Deposition Exhibit 17 makes reference to a meeting in December to set prices. What can you tell us about that meeting?"),

with the document-based questions
always coming at the end (unless the
authenticity or some other attribute of
the document itself is in question).

2.8 What Use May Be Made of Prior Statements by the Deponent?

Prior statements by the deposition witness need
not be shown to her before questioning about the
statements at the deposition (FED. R. CIV. P. 30(c)
("proceed as they would at trial") and FED. R. EVID. 613
("need not show it to the witness")). Because the
examination and cross-examination at a deposition
are to proceed in the same manner as permitted at
trial (with two exceptions not relevant here), the
deponent, like the trial witness, does not need to be
shown a potentially "impeaching" prior statement.
At trial, opposing counsel would be entitled to see
the statement after its use; at deposition, a copy
should be provided to opposing counsel, either out
of courtesy or because local rules require it. Opposing counsel has probably already received the document, either in the initial required disclosure under
Federal Rule of Civil Procedure 26(a)(1)(A) or in
response to other document requests.

2.9 What Reference May Be Made to Testimony by Other Witnesses?

One deposition witness may be asked about the testimony given by another deposition witness (FED. R. CIV. P. 26(b)(1)). Once again, there is nothing in the rules that precludes asking one witness about the testimony of another witness, either to confirm the earlier testimony or to try to discover ways in which to challenge it. At trial, comment by one witness on the credibility of the testimony of another witness is curtailed, if allowed at all, because the credibility of witnesses is for the trier of fact, not other witnesses.[1] This rule does not apply at deposition, where only privilege, court orders, and mistreatment of the witness preclude questioning (FED. R. CIV. P. 30(c)(2)).

Nevertheless, a trial witness could be asked whether she agrees with another trial witness's description of a scene or of the modus operandi of an alleged attacker. This does not invade the jury's province, but merely gives them the story

---

1. *See* City of Keller v. Wilson, 168 S.W. 3d 802, 819 (Tex. 2005).

from different perspectives. At deposition, there is no trier of fact, so nobody's province is in danger of being invaded; furthermore, one deponent's criticism of another's testimony is "reasonably calculated to lead to the discovery of admissible evidence," as required by Rule 26(b)(1).

2.10 What Protection Is Provided to Secrets or Confidences?

A desire to maintain a secret or a confidence does not itself create a *privilege* that will preclude discovery by deposition (FED. R. CIV. P. 26(b)(1), (5), and 26(c)).

Information does not become privileged merely because its possessor wishes to avoid disclosing it. If the rule were otherwise, deponents would obviously answer far fewer questions.

Practice Comment

Federal and state laws have reasonably well-defined categories of information that are privileged against disclosure (although in many jurisdictions—including the federal system—both procedural, common, and codified substantive laws must be searched for statements of privileges, since privileges are often created as parts of new laws and are then not recorded in any "procedure" or "courts" title). Attempts to create new areas of privilege are consistently met with vigorous resistance in the courts. Unless the information sought to be protected is within an already recognized category, it will likely be fair game for discovery. The area of commercially sensitive information, like customer lists, trade secrets, and future marketing plans are often treated just as though they were privileged, except there seems to be a lower threshold for defeating the confidential treatment. Very often parties will enter a confidentiality agreement that provides protection for such information; other times, the court will order, on request, that such information be protected until the court orders otherwise on motion or that the information be released for the eyes of outside counsel only.

Having stated these general principles, however, we must also note that most courts approach the resolution of such disputes by employing a balancing-test analysis. Thus, counsel seeking discovery of material not covered by a recognized privilege is often asked, "Why do you need this information?" The court proceeds to balance that stated need against the claimed injury that would result from production. This approach incorrectly places the burden on counsel to justify production, rather than on opposing counsel to justify nonproduction.

The better approach is to require the party seeking protection from discovery to move the court, under Rule 26(c), for a protective order and to carry the burden of showing that the material is entitled to protection because it is within a recognized privilege or that its discovery is sought to annoy, embarrass, oppress, or unfairly burden its owner. Then have the party resisting discovery demonstrate that public or other policy is served by protection. This does not predict the outcome of such motions practice, but it does give put the burdens in their proper order.

2.11 What Protection Is Provided for Attorney Work Product?

Neither attorney work product nor other materials prepared in anticipation of litigation may ordinarily be obtained through discovery depositions (FED. R. CIV. P. 26(b)(3)). This rule is based on the adversarial nature of litigation in the English system and the desire to prevent one lawyer from benefitting from the diligence of another. It does not matter whether the material sought was created by the party or by the party's agents (counsel, consultants, insurers, etc.); the key is whether the material was prepared "in anticipation of litigation." As with discovery from nontestifying experts, discovery of materials prepared in anticipation of litigation may only be obtained on motion to the court by the party seeking discovery showing that undue hardship would result if disclosure is not ordered. Even on a showing of undue hardship, however, the rule requires the protection of what is usually called "core attorney work-product," which include the attorney's notes, diaries, plans, and so forth, which actually reveal her plans for the litigation.

Practice Comment

A complication arises when the provisions of Rule 26(b)(3), protecting against the disclosure of the mental impressions of a party's attorney (classically deemed "core work-product"), are read against the obligations in Rule 26(a) to disclose the materials "considered" by an expert. A previous split of authorities of this question was resolved in the 2010 amendments to Rule 26, which now provides protection for attorney communications with experts, such as discussions of drafts of expert reports, unless those communications involve facts that the expert has considered, assumptions that she has relied on, or matters concerning her fees.

One can anticipate litigation now being burdened by disputes on whether attorney-expert communications were "factual" (and therefore discoverable) or merely "theoretical" (where, for example, an attorney tells the expert why the attorney believes the case is important to the public; all of which would supposedly be nondiscoverable). If the courts are interested in assuring full discovery of those elements that might influence an expert's opinion and allow complete cross-examination, this new rule is hard to understand. Where an expert has considered information provided by the attorney and that information contains core work product, it would seem that the attorney can best protect her work product by not revealing it to the expert and, further, that there is no compelling policy favoring such disclosure to the expert. It seems most likely that the attorney is sharing this core work product with the testifying expert in an attempt to make the expert more sensitive to certain problems or weaknesses in the case—that is, to have an impact on the expert's testimony and to enlist the expert in shoring up certain areas with her testimony. Because of that possibility, and because of the deference accorded expert testimony by juries, full discovery should be allowed concerning such communications or the possibility of them. The rationale supporting the position of the amendment seems simply to be, "Enough, enough, no more expert discovery fights, OK?" Not a good change.

2.12 What Problems Should Be Corrected at the Time of the Deposition?

Objections are required to be made at a deposition to errors or deficiencies that can be corrected if the objection is raised at that time; if such objections are not made at that time, they are waived (FED. R. CIV. P. 32(d)(3)(B)).

Practice Comment

Certain objections must be raised as soon as possible after they are discovered: problems with notice, with the qualifications of the officer, with the administration of the oath, with the form of questions, with the deposition procedures (such as the placement of video cameras), or any other matters that if brought to the attention of the proper person could be corrected. (Incidentally, objections to the notice must be in writing.) The purpose of this rule is to prevent the enormous waste of time and effort that would result from "sandbagging" by a party who decides to wait until trial to bring up problems or objections that could easily have been handled during the deposition.

Some confusion exists among practitioners as to the scope of the word
"form" in the popular statement of the
rule's requirement that "objections to
the form of the question must be made
at the time or they will be waived." This
confusion would no longer exist if the
focus were instead on "can the problem
be corrected" rather than on "form."
For example, a compound question
suffers a clear defect of form; everyone
recognizes that failure to object would
result in waiver of this objection
because it is a problem that could have
been corrected. If there is no objection
made to a compound question at the
deposition, no such objection to that
question and answer will be allowed
at trial. In comparison, a question
calling for a witness's identification of
a photograph may be objectionable as
lacking foundation if there had been
no demonstration at the deposition
that the witness was familiar with the
scene in question and had a basis for

stating that the photograph "fairly and accurately" depicted the scene. Since any two professors of evidence will have at least three opinions on whether such foundation is a matter of form, deposing counsel should be guided by the fact that absence of foundation is something that could be cured at the time (that is, a court may well find later that it could have been cured); therefore, failure to raise this objection would constitute a waiver, regardless of whether reasonable people could agree that foundation is a matter of form. Simply put, because it is *correctable*, it is *waivable*—and this is the practical rule that should be used to determine whether to correct defects alleged in objections. In other words, counsel should read Rule 32(d)(3)(B) as though the boldface language was not included:

> An objection to an error and irregularity at an oral examination is waived if:

(i) it relates to the manner of taking the deposition, **the form of a question or answer**, the oath or affirmation, a party's conduct, or other matters that might have been corrected at that time . . . .

2.13 What Can Be Asked about the Expert's Opinion in this Case?

In deposing an expert, questioning regarding the opinions the expert intends to present at trial is wide open, with the exception of those areas of attorney work product that have been placed out of bounds by the December 2010 amendments to Rule 26(b)(4). Counsel should consider starting with, "What opinions have you formed?" in place of starting with credentials. Credentials are the information most easily discovered outside the deposition and the least likely to yield useful information, while the opinion is the most important thing to be discovered from the expert before trial. If time runs out, it is better to have omitted credentials than to have omitted opinions and their associated bases.

Whenever the expert has proceeded through some sort of analysis to come to her conclusions, and that is certainly true most of the time, the following five questions work well at deposition:

1. What did you do?

2. Why did you do that?

3. How did you do that?

4. What were the results?

5. How do those results relate to your opinion?

These questions take any expert through the analytic process and actually divide that process into three logical components: the process (what, how, results), the rationale (why), and the connection between the results and the opinion put forward. While this formulation predated *Daubert* and *Kumho Tire*—with their requirements that the opinion be the result of a reliable methodology and be relevant to the issues in the case—it relates directly to those requirements: to claim that her methodology was reliable, the expert should be able to articulate what she did, why she did it, how she did it, and what results she obtained. She also ought to be able to explain the logical nexus (as required by *Daubert*) between the results obtained and the opinion expressed. This last requirement protects us against an expert who correctly applies a reliable methodology (like addition of whole numbers), but then leaps from the correct results to unjustified conclusions: "Because I have found that 9 plus 7 equals 16, I conclude that the defendant engaged in collusive price fixing." At deposition, each of the five steps should be explored for each opinion—identify the opinion, then go to step one, step two, and so forth, finishing with asking the expert to connect the results obtained to the opinion expressed.

2.14 What Can Be Asked about the Expert's Opinions in Other Cases?

The expert's opinions in other cases in which she has testified at deposition or trial are normally a matter of public record. (Counsel who took the deposition may be willing to provide the transcript, especially if she thinks it went well from her perspective.) Questions can be asked about that testimony as long as that questioning and those opinions are reasonably calculated to lead to the discovery of evidence that is admissible in the instant case.

Practice Comment

As with prior writings and other statements by an expert, the expert's opinions in other cases should be examined to determine whether the methodology and results used in those other analyses were consistent with the methodology and results in the present case. If they are *inconsistent*, one or more of the fundamental *Daubert* criteria is violated: the methodology (or its application) may not be "testable" in the sense that repeated trials by this or another expert should not have yielded results that are inconsistent with one another.[2] A problem can arise

---

2.   Of the four nonexclusive criteria of reliability discussed by the Supreme Court in the *Daubert* case (peer review, known error rate, acceptance in the relevant scientific community, and testability—easily remember using the acronym of PEAT), the most evanescent is the last—testability. It actually contains two related, but distinct

when the expert is engaged in other matters that have not yet been resolved,

---

characteristics of a reliable methodology—the approach should be testable, so that the court can determine that the results obtained are objective and replicable, that is, not dependent on who conducts the procedures and consistent over a number of tries; and the approach should be falsifiable. Falsifiability requires that we be able to conduct a test to determine whether an opinion derived from the methodology is true or false. For example, a theological expert might hold the opinion that every person has a guardian angel, and she may have come to that opinion by a careful reading of numerous holy writings. We cannot think of a test, however, that would determine whether she is correct or incorrect. Therefore, her opinion is not falsifiable, and the court should count that failing as a factor weighing against admission of her testimony on this point (although no single factor, in and of itself, is automatically grounds for admission or exclusion). At deposition, the utility of the concept of falsifiability is that if the expert identifies her bases, she should logically agree that if enough—perhaps all—of those bases are negated or excluded, her opinion will not stand. If instead she insists that despite the assumed negation of all of her bases her opinion still holds, it is obviously not a falsifiable opinion, and therefore it should not be received. In the more likely case where the expert argues that the opinion retains some bases, the deposing attorney should concentrate on identifying the essential bases so that they can be the target for the most serious factual challenge at trial.

and she therefore feels that she may not talk about those matters and her opinions in them. Mere reluctance, of course, is not an adequate excuse for refusing to answer, but if that reluctance is based on a confidentiality agreement filed in the other case or on a court's order of nondisclosure, the expert may be caught between a rock and a hard place. If she talks in this deposition, she violates orders in that case; if she obeys orders in that case, she and her client may be subject to sanctions here. The resolution of this dilemma has several steps:

First, in preparation, the attorney presenting the expert should ask her about obligations to protect other opinions or work from disclosure and then seek relief in that other forum, if appropriate;

Second, if the topic comes up at the deposition without any warning during preparation, the defending attorney should explain the problem to opposing counsel and ask that the subject be deferred until a motion for a protective order may be ruled on by the court or relief can be sought in the court in which the restrictions are in effect;

Third, counsel should advise or direct the witness not to answer and then suspend the deposition to allow time to seek a protective order or guidance from the court in this case; and

Fourth, counsel in the instant case should contact counsel in the other case to determine the status of the orders in that case and the extent to which they wish to provide assistance or be heard in the instant case.

2.15 What Are the "Usual Stipulations"?

There are no generally accepted "usual stipulations." From city to city and state to state, the "customary stipulations" vary widely to the point where there really are none. Counsel will avoid misunderstandings if she politely declines to accept any "usual stipulations." A stipulation is, after all, a bilateral agreement, so usual stipulations cannot be forced on a lawyer. If opposing counsel requests the usual stipulations, counsel should merely say, "Let's just take this deposition under the Federal (or state) Rules of Civil Procedure, and if any stipulations are needed, we can deal with them when the need arises."

One stipulation that is often included on lists of "common stipulations" is that no objections need be made to avoid waiver, except those objections to form. This stipulation is dangerous, since it allows counsel to "sandbag" the process by remaining silent about nonform problems that could be cured. For example, abuse of the witness is not a form problem; under this common stipulation, defending counsel could therefore later claim that opposing counsel had abused the witness by shouting or pounding on the table, and the court could consider the objection, since it was not waived, even though it was not made at the time and it could have been corrected. (*See* the discussion in section 2.12, above, concerning the wisdom of focusing on whether a problem is curable, rather than whether it is a problem of form.)

2.16 What Questions Must the Witness Answer Despite Objection?

Witnesses must answer every question posed, even those to which an objection has been made, unless the witness or her counsel claims that the answer would violate a privilege or that the question is beyond a court order or that it constitutes a serious attempt to annoy, harass, or oppress the witness. Rule 30(c) states explicitly that testimony at a deposition is to be given "subject to" objections; in other words, objections can be made, but the testimony comes in anyhow, except in the very limited circumstances mentioned above. Where annoyance, harassment, or oppression is claimed as a basis for refusing to answer a question, the cases teach that the refusal is only justified if it appears that the main purpose of the question is to annoy or harass or oppress in more than a minor way.

2.17 What Must Be Supplemented in an Expert's Deposition?

A party whose expert has provided information in an expert deposition must supplement that information if it is or becomes incorrect or incomplete (FED. R. CIV. P. 26(e)(2)). This rule is referenced in and is parallel to Rule 26(a)(2)(E), which requires that the expert's report be properly supplemented; this makes sense, since the expert report was created as an aid to discovery, especially discovery by deposition of the expert.

Practice Comment

Obviously, insubstantial additions or changes do not require supplementation. So, for example, an expert who comes up with an additional analogy to explain her testimony need not supplement her deposition to add that analogy. However, an expert who thinks of an additional step that improves her methodology needs to supplement her deposition (and report). At many expert depositions, the expert will state that she has not completed her work and intends to continue reading—or evaluating or analyzing—perhaps right up until the trial. In such a case, deposing counsel is reluctant to rely on opposing counsel's evaluation of the importance of such additional work in the context of deciding whether supplementation is required. There is no harm in asking the expert at deposition whether she will agree to provide a supplement to her report covering any type of additional work that she does. Although this technically should not create any greater obligation to supplement than exists under the rules without such agreement, it may provide a basis for arguing to the court, under Federal Rule of Evidence 403, that it is unfair to allow the expert to testify about such additional work when she broke her own testimonial promise to advise counsel of that work.

2.18 What Must Be Supplemented in a Nonexpert's Deposition?

Nonexpert depositions need not be supplemented (FED. R. CIV. P. 26(e)(1) and (e)(2)). Federal Rule of Civil Procedure 26(e)(2) specifically discusses supplementation of expert depositions in the context of requiring supplementation of the expert report submitted pursuant to the "voluntary" discovery under Rule 26(a). There is no such discussion of supplementation of depositions of lay witnesses in Rule 30. (Nonexpert depositions are not taken pursuant to Rule 26, but pursuant to Rule 30.) Furthermore, Rule 26(e)(1) sets out the duty to supplement interrogatory responses, responses to requests for production, and responses to requests for admissions, but it does not mention deposition responses. Exclusion from an apparently exhaustive list is good evidence that the item was not intended to be included. The Advisory Committee's Notes present this same analysis. It is therefore concluded that no requirement is imposed on a party to supplement a nonexpert deposition.

2.19 What Corrections May Be Made to the Deposition (and When May They Be Made)?

The witness may make any changes to the transcript that she feels are necessary to make it accurately reflect her testimony. Rule 30(e) provides that the witness may make "changes in form or substance . . . ." This rule does not limit the permissible changes to errors made by the reporter, or to misstatements by the witness, or to situations of misunderstood questions. The goal is to obtain a more accurate transcript, and the remedy for overzealous correction would normally be through a new deposition of the witness or cross-examination at trial. (Correction to the point of destroying the value of the original deposition may lead the court to strike the corrections and allow the original to stand—an inadequate remedy, of course, in some instances—or to permit additional deposition at the expense of the deponent or her counsel). Therefore, if the question at the deposition was, "What color is your house?" and the witness's answer was, "Red with a white top," because she heard "car" instead of house and "car" was the subject under discussion, the witness could correct the transcript by changing "house" to "car" in the question, or by changing "red with a white top" to "white with green shutters" in the answer. Either one creates a more accurate deposition transcript, although changing the attorney's question may more likely provoke a request for additional deposition.

Of course, both the original deposition transcript and the errata sheet containing the corrections are available to use at trial, and if the witness attempts to frustrate an impeachment by claiming that she corrected the mistake, the cross-examiner may want to point out the circumstances under which such corrections were made—that is, the witness and her attorney reviewed the transcript and discussed the questions and answers, the significance of the claimed mistakes, and the proposed corrections. If comparison is then made with the procedure at the deposition, where the witness normally had to answer without consulting with the attorney, the trier of fact may come to believe that the uncorrected transcript is more accurate.

During preparation, witnesses should be told that there are actually six opportunities to make changes to the deposition transcript. In chronological order (and what normally may be the order of most effect), they are:

First, right after the witness misspeaks, at which point she can say: "I'm sorry. I think that I misspoke a moment ago. I should have said that the office opened in November, not December";

Second, at some later time, but still during the deposition, when the problem comes to the witness's mind, at which point she can say: "Yesterday I told you that I took charge of this project in 2012. In thinking about it overnight, I realize it was actually in 2013";

Third, in response to a quick, clarifying question by her counsel—"Excuse me, did you say 'outgoing shipments' or 'incoming shipments'?"— the deponent could say, "I think that I said 'outgoing,' but I meant 'incoming'";

Fourth, in response to follow-on questioning by her counsel when the opposing party has completed questioning;

Fifth, in the normal process of reading, correcting, and signing; and

Sixth, during trial, after impeachment with the deposition or after the deposition is offered as an opposing party's statement if the deponent is a party, at which point the witness can try to explain the inconsistency away as a mere mistake at the deposition. (This is probably the least satisfactory approach.)

2.20 What Are Legitimate Bases for Objection?

There is no definitive listing of legitimate objections at depositions because one can imagine an infinite number of problems that could arise that might affect the reliability of the transcript, ranging from complaints about conditions ("the room is too hot" or "the room is too cold"), to attorney demeanor ("you are speaking too loudly" or "you are speaking too softly"), to the topics being covered ("this question is in no way calculated to lead to the discovery of admissible evidence"). In general, some of the most common objections relate to:

- The process (to which objection must be made or it will be considered waived)— the notice, the reporter, the reporting process, the provision of transcript, the persons present, etc.

- The conditions under which the deposition is taken—too noisy, too drafty, too crowded, too late, too long, etc.

- The form in which the questions are asked—ambiguous ("When Jones and

Smith spoke, did he seem nervous?"); compound ("Did you go to the store and buy bread?"); complex, leading, misleading ("Have you stopped beating your dog?"); lacking foundation, repetitive, cumulative, argumentative ("You are just lying now to protect your best friend, aren't you?" repeated in the same or different words more times than necessary to obtain an answer); annoying, oppressive, harassing because of the demeanor of the questioner.

- The subject of the questions—privileged; beyond the scope of an order or stipulation or other limitation (like Rule 30(b)(6) specifications); or annoying, harassing, or oppressive because of the subject matter ("Let's talk about your family's illiteracy and your problem with dyslexia").

It is much easier to define improper objections:

- It is improper to make an objection that has as its purpose coaching the deponent in her substantive response ("Objection. There is no need to ask this deponent those same tired old questions. Everyone else has already told you that it was not a defect in the design of the product.").

- It is improper to make an objection that is suggestive ("Objection, but you can answer, if you know.").

- It is improper to make an objection that is argumentative (in a different sense than used in immediate previous list) ("Objection. That's a stupid question, and it was stupid when you asked it twenty times this morning.").

- It is improper to engage in speaking objections or to make objections that waste time and improperly frustrate the discovery process.

- It is improper to object on the basis that terms in the question are undefined. The deponent is free to say that she does not understand the question, and it is gamesmanship for counsel to insist that questions be framed so that she can understand them. This objection merely coaches the deponent to be unresponsive.

- It is suggestive, and therefore improper, to object that the deponent lacks sufficient personal knowledge to answer the question. If the deponent does not know the answer, the deponent is free to say, "I don't know."

- It is suggestive, and therefore improper, to object that counsel does not understand the question; if the witness understands it, it should be answered regardless of counsel's lack of understanding.

- It is improper to object that a particular question is an attempt to trap the witness; if there is nothing else wrong with the question, the fact that it poses a trap into which the witness might fall is not a reason to object to the question, it is a reason to congratulate the questioner.

- It is improper to object that the question assumes facts that are not in evidence. In a deposition, there are no facts in evidence because no evidentiary record is being created at deposition. Putting facts in evidence is the purpose of the trial. This objection actually amounts to, "Objection, the answer would provide new information," which, of course, is the whole idea. At a preservation (or de bene esse or "trial") deposition, however, where the transcript is being created between counsel and her own witness for use at trial, an objection to new material *in a question* might be made on the grounds that there is no foundation or that the new facts have not been established; this will prevent counsel from essentially creating her own record with a mere assent from the friendly witness.

- As discussed in section 2.7, a document need not be shown to the deponent to question her on a topic mentioned in the document; of course, if the questioning is specifically about the document (e.g., "Who signed the letter to Kobe Bryant? Was it Shaquille O'Neal?") and there is no particular purpose to a memory test, fairness probably suggests that the deponent be provided with the document. Otherwise, the witness says, "I really don't remember; it may have been Mary Smith," and then the document is shown to the witness anyhow.

2.21 What Sanctions Apply for Failure to Make Discovery at Depositions?

Under Rule 37, a motion may be made to compel discovery where a deponent fails to answer a question or an organization fails to provide a designee under Rule 30(b)(6). The attorney taking a deposition may suspend or adjourn the deposition before moving for such an order compelling answers (FED. R. CIV. P. 37(a)(3)(C)). The parties, or the party and the deponent, must make a good-faith effort to confer in an attempt to resolve the disagreement before such a motion is filed (FED. R. CIV. P. 37(a)(5)(A)), and the motion must include a certification that the conference has occurred or at least been attempted (FED. R. CIV. P. 37(a)(1)). If the motion is granted, or if the recalcitrant deponent provides the discovery after the motion is filed but before the court rules, the court can order the deponent, her attorney, or both, to pay fees and expenses to the moving party (FED. R. CIV. P. 37(a)(5)(A)). If the court determines that the discovery is not appropriate and therefore denies the motion, it may enter a protective order and may consider imposing fees and expenses against the party who sought the discovery. If there is substantial justification for seeking or resisting the discovery, fees and expenses need not be imposed (FED. R. CIV. P. 37(a)(5)(B)).

After an order has issued compelling discovery, any refusal to make that discovery can be treated by the court issuing the order as contempt of court. Parties and their agents and controlling officials may be sanctioned, regardless of where the deposition occurred or was to have occurred. In addition to contempt, the forum court can impose additional sanctions on a party for refusing to make discovery, including a refusal to answer deposition questions. The available sanctions include:

- the subject under discussion may be taken as established against the recalcitrant party;

- the recalcitrant party may be precluded from offering evidence on that subject or from supporting or opposing claims related to that topic;

- fees and expenses may be levied against the party or its attorney; and

- particular claims or defenses may be struck.

A recent amendment to Rule 37(b)(1) further clarifies that when a deposition-related motion is transferred from one court to another (usually from the forum court to the court where the deposition is pending), a violation of an order can be treated as contempt in either court.

CHAPTER THREE

WHEN

3.1 May Depositions Be Taken before the Complaint Is Filed?

A deposition may be taken before an action is filed on a showing that the action cannot at that time be brought (FED. R. CIV. P. 27(a)). This rule also requires showing that the action is one that could be brought in federal court, a statement describing the subject matter of the lawsuit and the interest of the person seeking discovery, the purpose of the discovery sought, the names and addresses of the potential adverse parties, and the names and addresses of the persons sought to be deposed with a description of the proposed testimony. The potential adverse parties must be notified of the application and the proposed discovery.

3.2 May Depositions Be Taken Pending Appeal?

A deposition may be taken pending appeal on a showing made to the district court that the perpetuation of testimony is necessary to avoid a failure or delay of justice (FED. R. CIV. P. 27(b)). If there has been a full trial at the district court level, there will be little need for additional depositions preserving testimony; both the pretrial depositions and trial testimony are available, and it would only be in the unusual case in which a new witness has been suggested that any post-trial deposition would be appropriate. However, where the district court has disposed of the matter on summary judgment, or on motion to dismiss, or in other circumstances where some interlocutory appeal may be permitted and substantial time may pass before an appellate ruling, then the need for further depositions can be readily imagined, especially depositions to preserve testimony (also called de bene esse or trial depositions) of witnesses whose ability to attend trial may change. Where an appeal is taken that seeks a new trial, depositions pending appeal may be warranted where undeposed witnesses did not testify, but may testify at a new trial.

These de bene esse depositions normally differ from discovery depositions because their goal is to capture the testimony of witnesses that the questioners would otherwise present at trial; in other words, they are analogous to direct examination. Therefore, the rules of direct examination—both the rules of evidence and the rules of persuasion—apply. Counsel should ask few leading questions; the story should be interesting and understandable, mostly chronological; the substantive and illustrative exhibits should be carefully interwoven with the testimony; and the needs of the trier of fact to understand, see, follow, and appreciate the testimony should be kept paramount. This handbook is intended principally to provide help with discovery depositions, and the subject of preservation depositions—effectively, direct examination—is not fully treated here.

3.3 When, after the Discovery Conference, May Depositions Begin?

According to Rule 26(d), depositions and other discovery may begin after the parties have conferred for the required discovery conference to discuss the issues listed in Rule 26(f). One of the main purposes of the current discovery rules is to compel the parties to make "voluntary" early disclosure of the basic documents and information in the lawsuit (the voluntary disclosure mandated by Rule 26(a)). The discovery conference is the mechanism chosen to initiate the subsequent wave of "involuntary" or adverse discovery.

Practice Comment

In federal cases, there appears to be little decrease in the time taken for pretrial discovery, and unbelievable amounts of time continue to be expended in convoluted pretrial behavior before a matter can be presented to a jury. These two facts are strong evidence that this "voluntary" discovery approach has not saved significant time or expense. The successful experience of the Eastern District of Virginia's "rocket docket" continues to support the conclusion, touted by that court, that setting an early and firm trial date is the single most important factor in moving civil litigation forward. This calendaring should be incorporated into the rules to apply to every civil case with only a few, limited exceptions. Settlements will be encouraged as parties realize the burden of preparation, and cases will be narrowed as parties realize the resources required to actually pursue all of the collateral claims that they originally included. Justice will prevail under this approach at least as well as it has under the approach of delaying trials until the subject matter has been forgotten and Bleak House has crumbled.

3.4 When May Testifying Experts Be Deposed?

Expert depositions may be scheduled by the parties to take place after any required expert reports have been filed (FED. R. CIV. P. 26(b)(4)(A)). If in a particular case expert reports are not required, depositions of experts may be taken when and if the parties agree, after the Rule 26(f) conference. Expert reports are to be provided at a time specified by the court or stipulated to by the parties; in the absence of order or stipulation, they shall be provided at least ninety days before trial (in the case of rebuttal reports, thirty days after submission of the report they rebut) (FED. R. CIV. P. 26(a)(2)(D)).

Practice Comment

Before the creation of this provision of the rule relating expert depositions to reports, the timing of expert depositions had been a matter of debate among experienced trial lawyers. One school of thought believed that an early deposition of an expert might "trap" that expert in preliminary opinions that were based on inadequate understanding of the facts; the danger was that the expert could polish the opinion testimony after the deposition and perhaps attempt to present unexpected testimony or additional support at trial. The other school believed that a late deposition of the expert would provide the clearest understanding of the opinion testimony that would have to be met in court, although it obviously gave the expert more time to prepare.

In jurisdictions where expert depositions may be held before any expert reports are filed (which makes little sense, because the reports were conceived as an aid to discovery) or where expert reports are not required, the most efficient approach to the timing of the deposition of an expert would seem to be to postpone the expert deposition until the expert, as well as the deposing party, has mastered the facts of the lawsuit, so that both sides are working from a solid base of information. The alternative—early deposition—is probably a remnant of the "ambush" approach to trial advocacy, where advantages were sought by trying to catch the other side unprepared.

The underlying premise for the rules requiring expert reports is that expert depositions may be greatly simplified and shortened and considerable expense avoided if written reports are exchanged before the depositions. Many administrative agencies have long required written expert reports to be presented before trial, often substituting those reports for direct examination. This practice coincidentally confers considerable advantage on the cross-examiner. However, the purpose of the current rule is not to eliminate live direct testimony.

It also remains to be seen whether, having received a complete report under Rule 26(a)(2)(B), practitioners will engage in more limited deposition discovery of experts or will merely use the report as more fuel for their fires, conducting a deposition on everything that they would have before any reports were required, plus then deposing on the report. No marked decrease in the time spent on expert depositions had been noted before the requirement that all depositions conclude within seven hours was introduced. (Many counsel in complex litigation routinely stipulate that expert depositions may extend for two or even three days.) Logically, since the seven-hour rule accomplished directly what the expert report rule was supposed to accomplish indirectly, there is little reason to continue expert report practice. It may be that courts themselves are finding the reports helpful in understanding the expert portions of the case or in ruling on *Daubert* and other challenges to experts.

Observation by the authors suggests that reports confer no time-saving efficiencies in expert discovery.

3.5 When May You Get Some Priority for Depositions?

There is no priority conferred on a party's proposed schedule for a deposition because it was noticed first (FED. R. CIV. P. 26(d)(2)(B) and 30). Early in the life of the federal rules, there was a belief—which according to folklore hardened into an accepted practice in some areas—that being the first to file a notice for deposition earned that party some "priority" for that deposition, if not for the party's entire discovery program. In other words, no deposition by the other party could be taken before the first-noticed deposition was concluded. (Indeed, this concept of priority extended to other areas of discovery, so that one party was thought not to be obligated to answer interrogatories until its own earlier interrogatories were answered, regardless of the basis for the delay in answering.)

In reality, the need to accommodate the schedules of witnesses and counsel makes such a "priority system" completely senseless and impossibly cumbersome. All discovery could come to a halt because of the unavailability of a particularly busy (or evasive) witness. The clear rule today is the sensible one: discovery proceeds simultaneously, and the scheduling of depositions depends on the availability of witnesses and counsel, not on antiquated notions of priority. Of course, where one party is being entirely recalcitrant in refusing to make discovery, the frustrated party may apply to the court for a protective order, and such an order may preclude discovery by the procrastinating party until the court is satisfied that the problem has been resolved (or may impose an order leading to even more severe sanctions under Rule 37).

3.6 When Should Depositions and Returns on Requests for Production of Documents Be Scheduled?

There is no rule-based coordination between these two activities—collecting documents and taking depositions—but there is a logical sequence, based on the fact that one of the most important uses of depositions is to discover what the documents *did not* tell you. Young attorneys must learn to read between the lines of documents to identify what has not been written. That process (along with the normal process of determining what needs clarification and explanation in documents) takes time. Therefore, even with nonparties from whom documents must be obtained by subpoena, the document return should be scheduled sufficiently in advance of the deposition to allow time to analyze the pertinent documents—those from the witness's department, those with the witness's signature, and those dealing with matters within the witness's responsibilities. Where there are merely several hundred documents, an interval of two or three weeks before the deposition may be sufficient; in an antitrust, financial fraud, securities, environmental, or other massive document case, two or three months or perhaps substantially more time may be necessary.

3.7 When May Formal Corrections Be Made to the Deposition?

If requested by the witness or a party during the deposition, the witness has the opportunity to make changes in the form or substance of the deposition until thirty days after the transcript is available (FED. R. CIV. P. 30(e)). (There are many other, less formal opportunities for correction, and those have been written about in section 2.19, above.)

The deponent or the parties should request that the deponent be given thirty days after the written transcript is available to read the deposition, make changes in form or substance, and then sign the transcript or errata sheet. If no one requests that opportunity, the transcript will be treated as though read, corrected, and signed at the end of the thirty days. If the opportunity is requested by someone, but the witness then refuses to sign (whether the transcript has been read and corrected or not), the deposition will also be treated as signed after the thirty days.

One question regarding waiver of the right to read, correct, and sign remains: "Why would anyone want to waive having the witness read and correct the transcript?" Counsel taking the deposition is probably better off being able to say, in court, "You had a chance to read and correct any errors in this transcript before you signed it, didn't you?" Counsel taking the deposition would also like to know whether the deponent is going to claim that there have been mistakes in the transcript in matters of substance and would like to have the witness's signature under the phrase, "I have read the above transcript of my deposition, and it is true and correct to the best of my knowledge and belief," to strengthen any impeachment. Therefore, questioning counsel should not waive.

Counsel defending the deposition and the witness should both be concerned about misstatements or mistakes in transcription. The only reason for waiving, or not requesting reading, correction, and signing, appears to exist in a situation where fewer than thirty days remain until the anticipated use of the deposition either at trial or in support of a motion or response, where defending counsel is trying to squeeze deposing counsel out of a legitimate use of the deposition. A request for an order from the court could cure this difficulty. Normally, counsel defending the deponent should request the opportunity for the witness to read, correct, and sign. The transcript may be inaccurate; the deponent or others may be accurately reported, but they may have misspoken; or there may be problems that will affect the use of the transcript that need to be corrected. If defending counsel had been given a written statement, purportedly from his client, and asked to stipulate that everything in it was satisfactory to the client, counsel would never really agree without reading the statement and consulting the client. The analysis is the same with a deposition. Therefore, defending counsel should not waive.

3.8 When May You Take a Break?

There is no rule that states that breaks must be taken by mutual agreement.

It would be completely impractical to expect attorneys to agree on when breaks are appropriate—it is too inviting an opportunity for gamesmanship. Seeking agreement would be the same as seeking permission, and that would be denied whenever the opposition thought he could gain an advantage. Therefore, there is nothing that can be done to "deny" a break as a practical matter if the deponent or opposing counsel asks for one. If defending counsel requests a break, and questioning counsel says, "Let's go on for a bit," defending counsel can still get up and take the deponent by the elbow and leave the room for a reasonable break. Counsel that hired the reporter and noticed the deposition may control the record and even the location, but he does not control the bodies of the deponent and his counsel. Reasonable breaks will be allowed; they do not count in the deposition time; and disagreements about deposition timing are not the stuff that counsel wants to present to the court.[1]

---

1. *See* Blackmon, et al. v. Board of County Commissioners, 2011 U.S. Dist. LEXIS 13871, 2011 WL 663195 (D.C. Kansas, Feb. 14, 2011). The court had allowed eight hours for each deposition, and then, on motion, extended the times to allow questioning on additional, late-delivered documents, and to include the hours that had not been used for each deponent on the first day. This last adjustment seems to directly contradict

---

Practice Comment

However, counsel could attempt to persuade the witness to answer just a few more questions in the area or to wait through five more minutes of questioning before a break. Perhaps the witness and his counsel will get up and take a break anyhow, but the deposing attorney loses nothing by trying. A reasonable request to postpone a break for five minutes, even if unsuccessful, creates a record that may be helpful if the deponent and his counsel routinely abuse the right to take breaks and a protective order must be sought.

If a deponent returns from a break and has an altered recollection of the facts he was being

---

the language of Rule 30(d)(1), which reads, "one day of 7 hours." While it seems reasonable that a deposition begun in an afternoon may be adjourned and resumed the next day, it seems unreasonable that a party may end a deposition, bank the "remainder" of the seven hours, and call the witness back at some later date.

questioned about, counsel is free to ask whether anything discussed outside caused the witness to change his testimony as well as ask what was discussed outside. You may not get any useful answers because a claim of privilege is likely, but there is little cost to asking.

3.9 When Do Depositions Begin and End?

There is no rule on the time of day a deposition must begin or end. By convention, depositions tend to start at 9:00 or 9:30 a.m. and then proceed with appropriate breaks for coffee and lunch until 5:00 p.m. or so. The specific times are left to agreement of counsel. However, Rule 30(d)(1) limits depositions to one day of seven hours, absent a court order or written stipulation of the parties. Therefore, if a deposition starts at 9:00 a.m., and lunch is an hour, and there are two fifteen-minute coffee breaks, the deposition must conclude by 5:30 p.m. If the parties *agree* to break for the day at 4:00 p.m., an hour and a half could be held over for the next day or another agreed-on date. Without agreement, such a 4:00 p.m. break by the questioner may end the deposition.

(*See Blackmon*, note 3, this section.) The court "must" allow additional questioning time on a showing that someone (other than the taking attorney) or some circumstance has hindered the deposition or wasted time in some way.

Practice Comment

Because attorneys were perceived by courts to have abused the deposition process, and because courts (even magistrate judges) refuse to deal with routine discovery disputes because they are time consuming and frustrating in their recurrence, the U.S. Supreme Court and Congress have imposed this draconian seven-hour rule. Attorneys who are more capable at taking depositions will be more successful (that is, learn more information) in those seven hours than less skilled opponents, but attorneys who are skillful at disrupting the flow of legitimately discoverable information may profit even more. It may be that faced with this additional limitation on their trial preparation, attorneys may go to court more often for protective orders and motions to compel to protect the reduced opportunity that they have—an undesirable result.

If counsel has not completed his intended areas of examination by the end of the seven hours, and he reasonably believes that the fault lies with opposing counsel or the witness, he should note that concern on the record at the end of the deposition and ask opposing counsel to agree that he should have more time for questioning. If the opposing parties can agree that the seven hours was not sufficient, such agreement could be put on the record, amounting to a written stipulation, and a time and date could be established for the continuation of the deposition. If that request for additional time is denied, then he should explicitly reserve his right to seek additional deposition time from the court. He could seek an order under Rule 30(d)(2) for additional time; an order under Rule 37(d), compelling additional testimony from a party or the party's designee; or an order under Rule 45(e), to a nonparty witness to show why he should not be held in contempt.

If the parties anticipate, perhaps at the time of their Rule 26(f) conference on discovery, that certain depositions (such as expert depositions) might require more than seven hours—or might even require multiple days—a written stipulation to that effect would serve to extend the deposition periods. (It is assumed that the extensions would be reciprocal.) The parties do retain the power to behave reasonably; it is just no longer expected by the courts.

CHAPTER FOUR

WHERE

4.1 Where Must Depositions Be Taken?

A deposition may be set for any location where the witness can be compelled to attend and answer. To compel a witness's attendance at a deposition, the court enforcing the compulsion must have in personam jurisdiction over that witness so that sanctions may be imposed for failure to attend or failure to answer. A forum court in Iowa may not control the behavior of a mere deponent in New York; some other status than mere witness, like managing agent of a party, would have to be involved to subject that deponent to the power of the foreign forum court. Of course, once a witness agrees to attend at a particular location and does in fact show up at that location, even if that location is distant from the witness's home or office, the witness has submitted to the jurisdiction of the district court whose territory includes that location. For these purposes, expert witnesses are treated just like officers or managing agents of the party, so they can be compelled to appear in the forum—or in their home or office district—at the choice of the party taking the deposition. To hold otherwise would create difficulties, since the party chooses the expert and could pick one in Hawaii for a case filed in Vermont in an attempt to impose unacceptable costs on the opponent. In that case, the expert will likely be directed to appear for deposition in Vermont, absent a showing of such circumstances that justify deposition in Hawaii. Of course, telephone depositions can avoid such costs in the case of nonexpert witnesses who cannot be compelled to travel much beyond their home districts.

4.2 Where May Party Witnesses Be Deposed?

A deposition of officers or agents of a defendant corporation, or of an individual defendant who is beyond the process power of the forum district, must normally be taken in the district of the deponent's office or residence. The basis for this practice is that the plaintiff chose the forum. If the corporate officers conduct the company's business (which is at least in some way related to the lawsuit) within the forum, the court may order the depositions to occur in the forum. Nonforum corporate plaintiffs may be deposed in the forum, since they chose it, or in the district where they conduct their business or have their main offices. Designees under Rule 30(b)(6) can be deposed in the district where the organization resides, or in the district where the designee resides or has her office, or in the forum jurisdiction if the organization is located there (at the deposing attorney's option). Of course, all deponents may also be deposed wherever they and counsel for both sides agree, and the court in that district then has power over the witness (often simultaneously with the forum court).

4.3 In the Forum, at Whose Office Is a Deposition Held?

Your place or mine? A deposition may be noticed for the deposing counsel's office, a conference room in another firm's offices, an available courthouse room, the deponent's place of business, or even the witness's home or hospital room if the circumstances warrant and the witness can be compelled to attend.

4.4   Where Does Everybody Sit?

There is no rule controlling who sits where at a deposition. The deponent is not required to sit next to the reporter or across from the questioning attorney. The reporter, despite her insistence, is not in charge of where people sit. The reporter is a hired employee of the attorney noticing the deposition, and in matters not affecting the integrity of the record, she is subject to the reasonable direction of that attorney.

Practice Comment

Normally, counsel defending the deposition sits next to the deponent, ideally between the deponent and the reporter so that counsel remains involved in every question and answer. Questioning counsel sits across from the deponent. Questioning or defending counsel may stand, walk around, or even look out the window while questioning or defending, although none of this behavior is recommended as a general matter. The only limits on this "where can everyone be?" question are those imposed by the requirements that the witness not be subjected to attempts to annoy, embarrass, or harass her, and the reporter and video must be able to hear or pick up the questions and answers (and any comments intended to be included in the record).

4.5 Where Do Subpoenas Issue From?

Subpoenas to nonparty deponents issue from any court in the district in which the deposition is to be held and the witness resides or has her office, or any court within 100 miles of the location of the intended deponent, which is the limit on service of process (FED. R. CIV. P. 45(b)(2)). The simple concept is this: the deponent has to be subject to the issuing court's personal jurisdiction so that the court can compel attendance and discovery.

4.6 Where Do Protective Orders Issue From?

Applications for protective orders (or resolution of disputes arising during the deposition) may be made either to the forum court or to the court issuing the subpoena for the witness's attendance (FED. R. CIV. P. 30(d)). This is for the logical reason that the order will be directed to the parties' counsel, not to the witness, and the forum court has control over the behavior of counsel. By similar logic, as noted in the immediately preceding paragraph, orders compelling deposition testimony by a nonparty witness would issue from the court that issued the process compelling attendance, and orders compelling discovery from a party could issue from the forum court or the court for the district where the deposition takes place. To avoid confusion and contradiction, the nonforum court may defer to the forum court on questions of discovery against a party.

4.7 Where Do Orders to Terminate or Resume Issue From?

Under Rule 30(d), when a deposition has been terminated by the nonforum court where the deposition was being held, that deposition may be resumed only on order of the forum court.

4.8 Where Are the Notary and Reporter in a Telephone Deposition?

The notary must be located at the same location as the deponent so she can certify the transcript of the deposition as containing the words of the deponent; the reporter must be located at the same location as the deponent so she can identify the answers as those of the deponent. Questioning counsel can be at a remote location, or connected by telephone or video hook-up, but she should recognize that she is trusting to the circumstances and the honesty of defending counsel not to coach the witness because they may not be in her sight.

4.9 Where Do the Documents Go When the Deposition Is Finished?

Documents introduced as exhibits at the deposition are normally attached to the deposition transcript, if one is prepared, and returned with it to the attorney who noticed the deposition (FED. R. CIV. P. 30(f)(1)–(2)). If no transcript is prepared, the parties may agree on the handling of the exhibits or the reporter will retain custody. If originals were produced, copies may be substituted after parties have had a chance to examine the originals. This is not much of a problem today, since all parties have their own copies of virtually all documents used at a deposition; they are usually given additional copies by questioning counsel at the deposition; and all photographic or similar copies are defined as "duplicate originals" by Federal Rules of Evidence 1001–04, and are as admissible as the original.

Practice Comment

Numbering Exhibits

Exhibits should be marked with and referred to by unique identification numbers whenever they are used at a deposition. There are two common ways (and one uncommon way) to mark deposition exhibits: 1) mark them in the order in which they are used in the particular deposition regardless of whether they have been or will be used in other depositions; for example, Jones Deposition Exhibit No. 17, followed by Jones Deposition Exhibit No. 18, and so on.; or 2) mark them the first time they are used, like Jones Deposition Exhibit 1, and then refer to them by that same number in subsequent depositions of other witnesses. The advantage of the second method is that it completely avoids any ambiguity because no exhibits have the same number. A third method has the parties mark the exhibits with the same number or letter that will be used at trial, although the court must be willing to tolerate gaps in the number sequence at trial because many are culled, and few are chosen.

CHAPTER FIVE

WHY

5.1 Why Take Depositions of Your Own Witnesses?

Depositions of your own witnesses obviously do not (or should not) constitute discovery. You take their depositions because you have a concern that they will not be available for trial and you do not want to lose their testimony or have it available solely in the adversarial form of deposition by the opposing party. Own-witness depositions are taken where favorable witnesses are beyond the reach of the trial court and are unwilling to show up for the trial; where they are sick or of advanced age and may not comfortably be available for trial; where they are subject to some control, like the military, which may prevent them from being available for trial; or where their lifestyle or livelihood involves them in extensive travel, like archeologists, popular expert witnesses, and astronauts.

Normally, "preservation" or "trial" or "de bene esse" depositions are video recorded, unless there is something substantially unattractive or irritating about the witness's demeanor. In preparation for the video-recorded deposition, counsel has the witnesses rehearse their presentations of charts and drawings and physical exhibits and documents, just as he would for direct examination, and counsel presents them at the deposition just as he would for direct examination. If you would have them come down from the stand at trial to illustrate their testimony using magnetic cards stuck to a board to create a timeline, then you should do that at the deposition; if at trial you would have them draw a curve representing the decline in output from the failing steel company, then have them do that at the preservation deposition. All the visuals, all the exhibits, all the testimony is captured by the sponsoring attorney to display later at trial.

The desire to use the witness's testimony for motions practice is an inadequate reason to depose a favorable witness. Declarations are routine support for motions practice today, especially for summary judgment. With undeposed witnesses or in areas beyond the deposition, declarations may be entirely sufficient to raise genuine issues of material fact or to support the reliability to the expert's challenged methodology.

However, where your witness has been questioned by the other side in a discovery deposition and his deposition is likely to be used to support the opponent's motion for summary judgment, you may not be able to dispute that deposition testimony with a subsequent declaration. A court may consider a contradictory or explanatory declaration to be an attempt to sandbag the opponent's deposition efforts. You may want to notice your own deposition to preserve testimony. In summary, the reason to depose your own witnesses in this circumstance is to make certain that necessary testimony, or at least effective and persuasive testimony, is not lost for pretrial or trial.

5.2 Why Should You Use Depositions to Support Motions Practice?

As mentioned in the preceding section, declarations of your witnesses may very well not be permitted by the court to contradict their deposition testimony when that testimony is being used by your opponents to support their motions for summary judgment. This means that "sandbagging" at a deposition, allowing the full story to go untold, has substantial risks, since that deposition story may be all that the court hears. Today, approximately 95 percent of all cases filed, in both state and federal courts, are resolved without going to judgment or verdict: by settlement, on the pleadings, through summary judgment, or by other nontrial procedures. Neither the judge nor the jury may ever get to hear your witnesses live and in person.

The information that forms the basis for the greatest part of these nontrial resolutions comes from the depositions and the documents. Indeed, in *Kumho Tire Co. v. Carmichael*, 526 U.S. 137 (1999), the entire case was resolved on a motion premised on the opposing expert's deposition, where he indicated that he had not in fact used the methodology that he was describing as reliable. The trial court excluded the expert and then concluded that the plaintiff could not prevail without an expert and dismissed the plaintiff's case with prejudice. (The time had passed for naming additional experts.) "Affirmed," said the Supreme Court.

5.3 Why Do Depositions Help Uncover New Information Better than Interrogatories?

Depositions help counsel learn new information because they allow you to examine the basis for witness testimony very quickly and efficiently. At a deposition on oral examination, the witness can be asked, "Why did you cross in the middle of the block?" If the witness then answers, "Because I needed to get to the other side," the lawyer can, in a matter of only a few minutes, ask "why" and "what alternatives were there" and "who else was crossing there" and "what was your past experience in crossing there" and "what did you think about the safety of crossing there," and on and on. With open questions and a deponent across the table, the questioner can learn more in five minutes of deposition questioning than he can in several thirty- or sixty-day rounds of interrogatories and requests for admission. The immediate follow-up that is available at depositions provides a flow of information, and the questioner can make judgments to follow this or another clue, to return and follow another, to drill more deeply here, to explore more broadly there, all without waiting for weeks to receive a confusing mixture of objections, partial responses, and carefully worded evasions, all filtered through the mouth of the opposing lawyer.

5.4 Why Do Depositions Help Confirm Known Information?

Interrogatories can confirm known information, but they take too long to process—that is, to create, send out, read on return, and understand. Interrogatories involve challenges and objections and logical inconsistencies that require further interrogatories to resolve. With depositions, a few questions to a deponent sitting across the table can confirm what counsel thought he knew or can provide a clue about what the truth really is. They can also be used to put information from multiple sources into shorter, cleaner, single-source question-and-answer pairs that make very nice support for motions practice and settlement discussions.

5.5 Why Are Depositions Useful to Support Settlement Discussions?

Depositions are useful to support settlement discussions because the other side, especially the client, may never have looked at their witnesses with quite the same eye that deposing counsel has. Depositions, especially video depositions, may show the opponents another side to their case—the lying or evasive or unattractive demeanor of their witnesses, the unbelievable attempted explanation for the damaging document, the inconsistent story being told by the underlings—that they have not fully considered. A "settlement presentation" of selected deposition video clips, damaging documents, and persuasive argument may be what the opposing attorneys need to move their client off its position of intransigence. As a matter of client politics, they cannot appropriately create and present that material themselves to a valued client—at least, not easily. But they can certainly report on how opposing counsel intend to make use of the unflattering depositions of their important witnesses at trial.

5.6 Why Are Interrogatories and Requests for Admission Inferior to Depositions?

In complex commercial litigation today, months can be spent waiting in vain for responsive answers to interrogatories or for resolution of objections to interrogatories and requests for admission. Furthermore, at a deposition, in one morning the deposing attorney may ask 300 questions on a variety of topics, as he decides that he needs explanation and follow-up. In comparison, if 300 interrogatories were sent out, that number by itself would be a valid basis on which to quash or limit them.

Responses to requests for admission can result in the simplification of trial issues where matters are unambiguously admitted or denied; unfortunately, attorneys have difficulty asking questions that avoid the possibility of ambiguous responses, and even more difficulty in answering them. Such questions have to have a single fact as their focus, without qualification, modifier, or intensifier—very difficult for contentious lawyers. While the "admitted" part is attractive, attorneys should remember that anything said, at any time, in deposition or elsewhere, by the opposing party constitutes an "admission," now styled by the rules as an opposing party statement, and, if it is relevant, it should be admitted into evidence by the court at trial without further foundation and without a witness on the stand. Thus, the single attractive characteristic of interrogatories and requests for admission is, under the rules of evidence, also available at party depositions.[1]

5.7 Why Should Counsel Taking the Deposition Avoid Arguing with Defending Counsel?

Counsel's *primary* goal in taking a discovery deposition is to gain new information; the *secondary* goal is to confirm useful old information; other goals may be to assess the opposing witness, to advance settlement, and to determine

---

1. Here, "party depositions" include most Rule 30(b)(6) depositions, where designees provide testimony; depositions of officers, board members, managing agents, and others authorized to speak for the party; and depositions of agents or servants on matters within the scope of the relationship; and depositions by co-conspirators during and within the scope of the conspiracy (FED. R. EVID. 801(d)(2)).

whether the other side is seriously preparing for trial. None of these goals is served by spending time arguing with opposing counsel or advising him of counsel's theories about why something is relevant. Especially with the imposition of the seven-hour rule, deposition time is precious. But much can be accomplished, even in seven hours, if the time is spent efficiently asking open questions, following up those answers, exhausting the witness's knowledge, confirming known information by asking the witness if he agrees with it, recapping or summarizing, and testing theories.

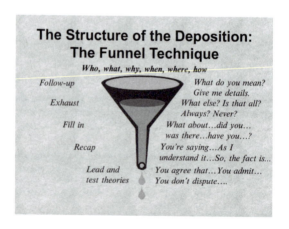

The Structure of the Deposition: The Funnel Technique

Who, what, why, when, where, how

Follow-up	*What do you mean? Give me details.*
Exhaust	*What else? Is that all? Always? Never?*
Fill in	*What about…did you… was there…have you…?*
Recap	*You're saying…As I understand it…So, the fact is…*
Lead and test theories	*You agree that…You admit… You don't dispute….*

To the extent that counsel conducting a deposition spends time in colloquy with opposing counsel—arguing relevance, asked and answered, foundation for a question, whether he has a right to direct the witness not to answer, or any of the other hundred things that defending counsel come to the deposition armed with—deposing counsel is not accomplishing any of his important goals, and defending counsel knows that. Experienced attorneys know enough tricks that they are able to keep less-experienced attorneys completely tied up in knots, frustrated at their inability to obtain new information, but unwilling to resist the bait of a good argument or stupid objection. The game has been played by defending counsel since 1936 (the year the Federal Rules of Civil Procedure were issued), and probably before (since we have been using depositions in this country since the Revolution and before[2]). Opposing counsel will continue to play this obstructionist game successfully until deposing counsel realizes that the answer to that

---

2. *See, e.g.,* various depositions referenced in the Hamilton Papers, Nos. 95154—55, cited in J. GOEBEL & JOSEPH HENRY SMITH, LAW PRACTICE OF ALEXANDER HAMILTON (Columbia Univ. Press, 1969).

tactic is within their own grasp: ask a question, get an answer, ask another, focus on the witness, ignore opposing counsel, ask another question, and keep on going.

CHAPTER SIX

HOW

6.1 How Do You Notify the Witness to Appear?

To schedule a deposition and obtain the witness's presence, issue a notice to a party under Federal Rule of Civil Procedure 30(b)(1) or a subpoena to a nonparty under Rules 45(a)(1) (A) and 45(a) (2). If the witness is not a party, but closely associated with a party (like a managing agent, officer, or director), they can be noticed like the party. Normally, counsel will confer on dates and agree that subpoenas are not necessary for any employees of a party, regardless of their place in the hierarchy. A nonparty witness should be called by telephone before a subpoena goes out, since compulsory process is by its nature aggressive. Demonstrate your willingness to cooperate in finding a convenient date, and that may pay dividends in how forthcoming the witness is at deposition.

6.2 How Do You Obtain Protection from Unreasonable Timing?

A challenge to the reasonableness of the time allowed between notice or subpoena and scheduled appearance of the witness to give deposition testimony is made by motion for a protective order (FED. R. CIV. P. 26(c)(1)) or by a nonparty target by motion to quash or modify the subpoena (FED. R. CIV. P. 45(c)(3)(A)(i)). A motion to quash a subpoena to a nonparty is made in the federal court issuing the subpoena, not in the forum court, unless they are the same (FED. R. CIV. P. 45(c)(1)).

The definition of a "reasonable time" will depend on all of the circumstances, including the convenience of the witness, the needs and locations of the parties, and the schedule of the trial. For example, if a party adds a witness to its case late in the pretrial process or during trial, the court may authorize a deposition on short notice; in such circumstances, if the witness is not available for such an expedited deposition schedule, the party seeking to call the witness might be precluded from doing so.

6.3 How Do You Protect Your Client from Improper Process?

If a witness has not been properly served, or the notice is unreasonably short, counsel should make a motion to quash the subpoena or to modify the notice with a motion for protective order in the court issuing the subpoena or in the forum court if the witness is a party or an agent of a party. While the rules indicate that the examination will proceed subject to objections to the process, conduct, or topics (FED. R. CIV. P. 30(c)(2)), this section clearly does not contemplate a situation where the notice is too short to allow the deponent to attend or where it provides the wrong date or address. In those circumstances, the deposition cannot go forward, and relief should be sought from the court by motion.

6.4 How Do You Start the Deposition?

There is no rule or set form for beginning a deposition. After the witness is sworn, many attorneys give the witness a lecture on the deposition process to create a record that may be used in a later impeachment showing that the witness understood the deposition process, that it was a fair process, and that she had counsel; other attorneys launch right into substantive questioning and insert particular instructions or directions when, and if, a problem arises. This latter approach is most efficient because many of the "beginning instructions" may never be needed. However, some instructions to the witness may be useful at the outset because this record may be used later, and it is persuasive to have the witness's agreement that this is not a star-chamber proceeding. However, with a party-witness, it is generally true that the defending attorney has given her witness thorough instructions about the deposition process, and it may be sufficient to ask whether the deponent has counsel and whether she has any questions about the process or her role.

Practice Comment

With a nonparty witness, it is probably best to start with standard deposition instructions, such as are found in just about every deposition reference book, including *The Effective Deposition* from NITA. At the least, ask the witness if there is any reason that she cannot understand and respond to questions; tell her that if she does not understand, she should say that; and ask whether she is taking any medications, prescriptions, or anything else that would interfere with her ability to provide testimony on that day.

6.5 How Should You Frame Questions to Obtain New Information Efficiently?

Ask open questions such as "who," "what," "when," "where," "why," "how," "tell us," "describe," and "explain" because they are more useful in discovery depositions than leading questions. Leading questions presume that the questioning counsel already has correct information. The goal in a discovery deposition, stated most simply, is to get the witness to talk about relevant topics, not to force counsel's views on her.

6.6 How Do You Use Leading Questions Effectively?

Leading questions—that is, questions that suggest or even state the answer within themselves—are used in discovery depositions to wrap up subject areas and close off opportunities for the witness to amend testimony later. For example, after a witness has answered the question, "Who was there?," she should be asked, "Was anyone else there?," and then, "Based on what you have told us, then, John, Mary, Paul, and Hermione were the only ones with you at the hotel walkway collapse, is that right?"

Counsel can also use leading questions to avoid confusion when moving the deponent (and everyone else) to a new topic. Counsel would say something like: "We have been talking about Barry Jones and his work as your assistant. You also had another assistant during that time, a woman name Amanda Norton, isn't that true? Let's talk about her work for a few moments."

6.7 How Can You Repeat Questions to Obtain Refined Answers?

There is no rule that precludes repeating a question, or rephrasing a question, or returning to an area of questioning in an effort to probe the consistency of the witness's responses. Counsel may not repeat a question solely to annoy or harass a witness, but seeking further information or refinement is neither of those. The questioning attorney can try the "reverse repeat" with a taciturn witness: "Is there anyone besides yourself who had access to those files?" "No." "So, absolutely no one else ever had access to those files?" "Well, when you put it that way, I suppose someone may have been able to get into them at some point."

Practice Comment

A serious difficulty for a lying witness is to remember what she has said; therefore, if you as questioning counsel believe that the witness is creating facts or adjusting her story, follow these practical suggestions:

➢ Ask for details in all areas where you suspect prevarication.

➢ After letting thirty minutes go by, ask for the same information using different questions.

➢ Ask for more details, such as the names of other people who were there, who know about the facts, who participated in conversations about those facts, who had to receive reports of those facts, or who had to take action based on those facts.

➤ Ask the witness to identify all documents that relate to those facts, but do not show the witness those documents (or other relevant documents) at the deposition, if there are clear inconsistencies.

6.8 How Should Deposing Counsel Control the Pace of the Deposition?

There are no rules regarding the pace at which counsel must ask questions at the deposition, other than she must refrain from harassing or annoying or oppressing the witness (FED. R. CIV. P. 30(d)(3) (A)). It would probably be actionably annoying if counsel waited fifteen minutes between an answer and the next question. But a one-minute pause while the questioner considers what to ask next or how to ask it, or a similar pause while she gives the witness a chance to tell more of the truth to fill the uncomfortable vacuum caused by the questioner's silence, is not actionable and may be quite productive.

Practice Comment

As a matter of lay psychology, you should generally ask questions somewhat more quickly after an answer when the deponent is being open and forthcoming and seems to need little encouragement to continue to speak—ask another open question and let the witness continue. If the witness is hesitant and guarded, it may help to give her a chance to add more by pausing before asking the next question—letting her think that you are happy to wait and that you do not believe that the witness is quite finished. Whether one or the other of these approaches works for a particular witness is something that you will have to experiment with; just be aware that there are at least these two alternatives.

6.9 How to Object to Opponent's Behavior?

Objecting is easy; making a useful record is more difficult. If counsel is defending a deposition, and her opponent, in questioning, is behaving in such a way that interferes with the deponent's right to have a clear record made of her answers, deponent's counsel should adopt a multistep approach: At the first and second instances, she should object and state the objectionable conduct ("Objection. Mr. Smith is pounding on the table"). At the same time, she should ask the reporter to mark those points in the transcript. On the third instance, defending counsel should make a more complete record ("Objection. Mr. Smith, you continue to raise your voice and pound on the table. I believe that you are trying to harass and intimidate Ms. Jones, the deponent. Please stop that behavior. If you do not stop, we may suspend this deposition to obtain a ruling from the court."). Counsel should also ask the reporter to mark that point in the transcript. At the next instance of such conduct, counsel should make the decision whether she wants to go to the court for a protective order or if she wants to continue; if counsel and her witness want to continue, counsel must consider whether she wants to bring in a videographer so the court can actually see opposing counsel's behavior, which probably (in this example) does not appear too offensive in the typewritten transcript. Counsel will often find that with a video camera rolling, the offensive behavior is almost certain to cease, and this is true whether it is deposing counsel or defending counsel who is misbehaving.

6.10 How Do You Make Designations of Transcript that You May Use at Trial?

Where deposition material is intended for use at trial, it is ordinarily "designated" and submitted to the other party for "counter-designation." This designation process is commonly covered by the local rules of the district court or by a standing pretrial order issued by the particular judge. A common procedure is to exchange a single transcript of the deposition testimony, with the offering party marking its designations in one color, the opposing party marking counter-designations in another color, and, if necessary, the parties marking "response" and "counter-response" in third and fourth colors. (Where the deposition was taken by video or sound recording, material submitted to the court for ruling on objections must be presented in the form of a written transcript (FED. R. CIV. P. 32(c)). The video is then edited in accordance with the court's ruling.) This provision makes it easier for the court to review challenged material in a non-stenographically recorded deposition. Where a party expects to use portions of non-stenographically recorded deposition testimony at trial for purposes other than impeachment, a transcript must be provided to the other parties in advance of trial (FED. R. CIV. P. 26(a)(3)(A)(ii)).

6.11 How Does Your Client Communicate with You during the Deposition?

Except in those districts that have adopted and retained strict (almost draconian) rules of deposition conduct, such as those found in Judge Gauthrop's decision in *Hall v. Clifton Precision*,[1] counsel may talk with the deponent during breaks in the deposition. Counsel may not coach the witness during those breaks any more than she

---

1. Hall v. Clifton Precision, 150 F.R.D. 525 (E.D. Pa. 1993).

could coach the witness at trial or any other time, but she may review procedural matters ("listen carefully to the questions"), and she may discuss whether there are matters that should be clarified by follow-on examination after the questioning counsel is through. During the preparation sessions before the deposition, counsel should explicitly tell the witness: "If you have any questions, turn to me and ask me. You can always talk to me. I can't tell you answers, but I can talk to you about all of the procedures at the deposition." Counsel should also make it clear to the witness during preparation that the witness should ask her about any concerns about privilege, privacy, or confidentiality at any time, either by turning away from the table so that opposing counsel cannot hear or by asking for a break. Once privileged information is spoken in public, the privilege is waived, so the witness needs to be aware of the opportunities to gain counsel's guidance on such matters.

6.12 How Do You Handle Exhibits at Deposition?

When counsel wants to show the witness an exhibit, she should take out sufficient copies so that there is one each for the deponent and defending counsel and any other counsel present. One copy per party is sufficient in multiparty cases. (Deposing counsel already has her own working copy.) Counsel then states, on the record:

> Mr. Deponent, I am giving the reporter a document with Bates Number 0003197 through 0003205, and I am asking her to mark it with the next Deposition Exhibit Number, which is 17.

> Mr. Reporter, after you mark Exhibit No. 17, would you please hand it to the witness.

> Mr. Opposition, here is a copy of that document for you.

> Now, Mr. Deponent, do you have Exhibit Number 17 in front of you? Please take your time and review the entire document if you want to, but I will first be asking you about the second paragraph on the first page. Let me know when you are ready for my question.

Many witnesses will only pay attention to the portion that counsel says she is going to ask about and perhaps scan the rest. Counsel defending the deposition should remind the witness in preparation to take her time when reviewing the document. At deposition, defending counsel should also postpone questions until the witness indicates that she is ready: "Counsel, would you please wait to ask your question until the witness has finished her reading of the document."

Documents introduced as deposition exhibits are normally attached to the deposition transcript, if one is prepared (FED. R. CIV. P. 30(f)(2)). As mentioned in an earlier section, usually all parties will have xerographic or photographic or electronic copies of the documents, which are as good as originals (FED. R. EVID. 1001-04).

6.13 How Do You Number Exhibits at Deposition?

The Practice Comment to section 4.8 describes in detail three ways to number deposition exhibits. No matter which way is used, or even if another is invented, the purpose is to eliminate confusion in the future about what document the witness was referring to as she gave answers. Where Bates numbers were stamped on each document, those should be referenced also to ease computerized database searches.

CHAPTER SEVEN

EXPERT DEPOSITIONS

7.1 What Is the Relationship between the Expert Report and the Expert Deposition?

The expert report requirement was created in an effort to simplify expert depositions and, perhaps, thereby to make them shorter and less expensive. As mentioned elsewhere in this handbook, however, it seems unlikely that giving trial lawyers more material to question an expert about will result in a shorter deposition.

Mechanically, the report must precede the deposition (FED. R. CIV. P. 26(b)(4)(A)), and the report must precede the trial by at least ninety days (FED. R. CIV. P. 26(a)(2)(D)), absent specific order from the court. The result is that expert depositions are often taken within the last ninety days before trial.

Practice Comment

The report must contain all the opinions and bases on which the expert will testify, so, in theory, it would seem automatic that opinions not in the report would not be permitted. Things are not so simple, however.

If deposing counsel asks about matters outside the report, such as additional opinions or other materials, it is illogical for him to claim that he is surprised or disadvantaged if the expert brings those opinions and bases up at trial. On the other hand, if no deposition questioning deals with additional opinions or bases, there is the possibility that the court will be persuaded that for one reason or another (perhaps the court sees a connection among them that counsel did not), those additional opinions or bases are admissible and the cross-examiner will be unprepared. The most sensible way out of this dilemma is for deposing counsel to ask the expert at deposition about the opinions and bases that the expert included in his report. Counsel should ask whether he intends to supplement or change his report in any way or whether it is final (as the rules require). After he admits it is final, counsel should ask questions about other areas, other opinions, and other bases, always confirming that "since this is not in your report, you do not intend to speak to it at trial, right?" This is probably the best that deposing counsel can do—the additional material is not in the report and the expert admits that he does not intend to supplement, so it should not be admissible; and yet counsel has learned something about it at the deposition, so he is somewhat prepared in the event the court rules that, for some reason, the expert can testify about it.

7.2 What Is the Most Important Question to Ask at an Expert's Deposition?

The most important question for counsel to ask, right at the beginning of the deposition after the preliminaries are out of the way, is: "What are all of the opinions that you have formed in this case?" Counsel should not rely on the expert's report to provide full disclosure; it will not reveal the robust discussion that the expert intends to bring to trial. Instead, deposing counsel should make the expert list his complete set of opinions right then, at the start of the deposition. Once counsel has the entire menu of opinions, you should go back to the ones in which you are most interested and drill down, asking about bases, methodologies, and the logical connections between the results from the methodology on the one hand, and the opinion presented on the other. When asking about the expert's opinions, you should make certain to exhaust the witness's information. If you say, "What are your opinions?," and the expert gives three right off the bat, you must make certain that there are not four, or five, or eleven. It is not the expert's job to volunteer information. And similarly with bases, alternatives, assumptions, and so forth, you should always ask: "Are there others?"

7.3 What Is the Most Important Preparation for the Expert's Deposition?

During deposition (and trial) preparation, the expert should be encouraged to identify the most important supporting arguments for his overall analysis; his four supporting columns or pillars; his three core concepts. Then, when he is pressed to explain why he did not consider this, or try that, or use this other methodology, or adopt a framework utilized by Copernicus, he should evaluate that challenge in light of the impact it has on his core concepts. If the challenge does not affect those concepts, that will be his answer; in scientific terms, his analysis is not *sensitive to* that other information. This quick litmus test helps the expert avoid overanalyzing marginally serious challenges. When he is asked patently irrelevant questions, or questions that misuse his terms of art or misstate his methodology, he can return to one or more of his core concepts and explain why those are sufficient to support his opinion, regardless of the misunderstanding by questioning counsel.

7.4 What Is the "Fourteen Document Rule," and How Do You Use It to Prepare Your Expert?

The "fourteen document rule" hypothesizes that the trier of fact cannot absorb more than fourteen documents in analyzing a party's case. No one can remember the chronology, authors, recipients, and topics covered by 114 documents, and they certainly cannot remember 1,114 or more. Why, then, would counsel want to put that many documents before the judge or jury? Therefore, the key is to reduce the important documents to "fourteen" or fewer. How can this be done? Counsel and the expert (or the lay witness, for this rule applies with them, too) should use summaries prepared by the witness; the lawyer must ask the key witnesses whether there are documents that summarize the plaintiff's recovery process while in the hospital; the expert, with the assistance of the litigation team, should create one-board illustrative exhibits that capture the thrust of the information from the three years of data entered by the accounts payable department. The choice is clear: counsel must find ways to simplify or be prepared for the jury or judge to misunderstand or give up. Federal Rule of Evidence 1006 allows such summaries to be used when the opposing party is given notice and opportunity to examine the underlying data.

7.5 How Protective Should You Be of the Expert at the Deposition?

Cross-examination of experts at trial is broader than allowed of the lay witness because experts have been given the privilege of stating their opinions while others are confined to the facts of what they saw, felt, heard, tasted, or smelled. The expert has only his credibility to sell, because the jury and judge are, almost by definition, incapable of evaluating the validity of the science behind the opinions.[1] For all of these reasons, you must allow the expert to develop his credibility

---

1. FED. R. EVID. 702. The rules allow experts to be presented when the expert will be of assistance to the trier of fact. Therefore, it is only when the trier of fact needs help with a topic that an expert may be used. If the trier of fact understood the subject matter well-if we all

by standing on his own two feet. In a case where substantial, but correctable damage is inflicted at the deposition, you can mitigate with follow-on questioning after opposing counsel has concluded. During the deposition, however, let the expert work through the questioning; it is what he will have to do at trial.

7.6 What Role Does Your Expert Have in the Deposition of the Opposing Expert?

Well before the deposition of the opposing expert, the expert (and his staff) should meet with the trial team and discuss the areas that require questioning at the deposition. A thorough analysis of the opposing expert's report is a necessity; the facts and data manipulation can probably be evaluated by the expert's staff; the selection and application of the methodology should be evaluated by the expert himself. All of them should be invited to provide questions to counsel, who should discuss those questions with them to make

---

understood astrophysics, then no astrophysicists would be allowed to testify in federal trials.

certain that he understands the ramifications of the various answers he may get. The expert should not attend the opposing expert's deposition because it is too expensive and only marginally useful compared with reading the transcript. Because the expert will rely, in part, on the testimony of the opposing expert and facts learned at trial, he will not be excluded under Rule 615, and he is therefore not logically precluded from reading the transcripts of the opposing experts' depositions.

7.7 What Is the Relationship between *Daubert*[2] and the Expert's Deposition?

There are two principal topics that must be covered during the deposition of an expert or other discovery: first, what opinions has the expert come to, and, second, what are the bases for those opinions; that is, what methodology and data were used to develop those opinions? With the increased focus on the reliability of expert opinions brought to bear by the *Daubert*

---

2.   Daubert v. Merrell Dow Pharmaceuticals, Inc., 509 U.S. 579 (1993).

case and its progeny, examination on the subject of the methodology must cover not only how the opinion was developed, but what evidence there is that following such a methodology is likely to result in reliable information.

For example, prior to *Daubert*, an expert might himself support the admissibility of his methodology by testifying that the approach had achieved general acceptance in the relevant scientific field, the old *Frye*[3] test. We would inquire at deposition about the methodology and about his belief that it was generally accepted, but if he persisted in that testimony at trial, then the court would likely receive his opinions into the record. This is the precisely the ipse dixit approach criticized by the U.S. Supreme Court in *Daubert*: just because the expert himself says a methodology is reliable or accepted does not make it so, and external evidence should be presented and examined.

With *Daubert*, a greater burden was placed on the proponent of the expert testimony, thereby providing greater opportunities for challenge

---

3. Frye v. United States, 293 F. 1013 (D.C. Cir. 1923).

by the opponent, and those opportunities must be identified in the expert deposition. Now we not only look to see, for example, whether the expert believes that the methodology is generally accepted (because a modified *Frye* standard is one of the criteria recommended by *Daubert*), but also for other evidence, beyond his testimony, that the field recognizes the methodology. Treatment of other criteria of reliability, including publication in peer-reviewed journals, known error rate, and testability and falsifiability, follows this same approach—we look beyond the expert's ipse dixit ("Yes, I believe that the error rate is acceptable"). We are looking to see if the claimed knowledge (a well-founded opinion) is actually that—it need not be absolutely true or beyond dispute, but there must be some indications that it is the result of processes that generally have been shown to lead to the truth. This is a problem of "authenticity" under the Federal Rules of Evidence—is this evidence what its proponent purports it to be?

In the following article, reprinted by permission of the authors, a number of criteria of reliability are examined, and for each a number of deposition questions are proposed so counsel can probe beyond the expert witness's ipse dixit. Of course, the Supreme Court has reminded us that the criteria for ascertaining reliability are as infinite as the fields of human knowledge, so there should be no misunderstanding that these topics and questions are offered as exhaustive. Instead, they are offered as a starting point for thought about the question, "How do we know when someone else actually knows something?" and the even more difficult question, "How do we know when *we* know something?"

THE *DAUBERT* DEPOSITION DANCE: RETRACING THE INTRICACIES OF THE EXPERT'S STEPS

By David M. Malone and Ryan M. Malone

After the decision in *Daubert v. Merrell Dow*[1] there was some question about whether the gatekeeping responsibilities of the federal trial courts extended to all expert testimony, or merely to "scientific" expert testimony. Even among circuits that believed that only scientific testimony was covered, there was confusion as to what was scientific testimony and what was "technical or other specialized" testimony. The *Kumho Tire*[2] case resolved that confusion, by clearly stating that the methodologies underlying all expert testimony must be evaluated for reliability.

---

1. *See* Daubert v. Merrell Dow Pharmaceuticals, Inc., 509 U.S. 579 (1993).
2. *See* Kumho Tire Co. v. Carmichael, 526 U.S. 137 (1999).

This decision therefore clarified the occasions for application of the *Daubert* approach, although it compounded any remaining problems by increasing the number of cases covered. Chief among those remaining problems is the need for trial practitioners and trial courts to develop a coherent body of analytic tools by which methodological reliability can be measured with some confidence by lawyers and judges without formal training in the specialized fields. For example, how does the trial judge assess the reliability of methodologies employed by the astrophysicist, since it is unlikely that the trial judge coincidentally has been trained in astrophysics.[3]

Although the Supreme Court in *Daubert* and again in *Kumho Tire* emphasized that the four

---

3. Some suggest that the court could overcome this problem by obtaining its own expert (at the parties' expense, of course). This is not a solution, however, because the question of the reliability of expert methodologies would then legitimately be directed toward the court's expert and her methodologies. Pundits might suggest that another court-retained expert could be consulted, and then another, until we complete some regression back to a Prime Expert.

criteria—publication in a peer-reviewed journal; known or knowable error rate; general acceptance in the relevant scientific community; and testability or replicability (including the concept of "falsifiability"⁴)—were not exclusive (indeed, none of

---

4.   A premise is "falsifiable" if it can be proven wrong, usually through direct experience. For instance, the premise "all ravens are black" is falsifiable, since it can be proven wrong by the discovery of a white raven. On the other hand, the premise "everything in the universe doubles in size for a second, and then it halves in size the next second" is not falsifiable, since it is impossible to disprove through direct experience. (If everything is alternating in doubling and halving in size, it remains relatively the same size, and therefore the difference is impossible to measure.) Scientific premises are tentative and falsifiable, while some other premises are not. It is common for creationists to point out that evolutionary biologists often contradict parts of evolutionary theory. However, the testing of evolutionary theory by its subscribers, which the creationists see as a weakness of that theory, is actually proof positive that the theory is scientific. *See, e.g.*, ROBERT T. PINNOCK, TOWER OF BABEL: THE EVIDENCE AGAINST THE NEW CREATIONISTS, xvi (MIT Press 2000): "Science imposes severe constraints upon itself to ensure that its conclusions are intersubjectively testable, constraints that require that it not appeal to supernatural hypotheses or allow the citation of special (private) revelations as evidence. The new creationists, including Johnson and philosophers such

the four is even required), there seems to be some belief among attorneys and judges that we must measure reliability by those is criteria alone. In an earlier article,[5] the authors suggested a number of additional, objective criteria that could be utilized in conducting this analysis, beyond those four mentioned in *Daubert*. Abstract criteria, whether four or fourteen, are not easily applied in discovery depositions, however, and we must recognize that it is in deposition that the foundation for challenge to an expert's methodology is uncovered. We therefore thought it might be useful to examine some specific questions that an attorney can ask at deposition to explore these various concepts of reliability, with follow-up and rationale explained as we go along.

---

as Alvin Plantinga, reject these constraints and share the view that supernatural explanations should be admitted into science."

5. *See* David M. Malone & Ryan M. Malone, "The Zodiac Expert: Reliability After *Kumho*," 22 THE TRIAL LAWYER MAGAZINE 265 (Fall 1999).

1. Publication in a Peer-Reviewed Journal

This criterion of reliability actually has two prongs to it: an article describing the methodology must have been published, which subjects it to scrutiny by whatever readership the journal has; and the article must have been reviewed, pre-publication, by "peers" in the particular field of knowledge, who ostensibly would scrutinize it for errors and challenge any unsupported conclusions. It is objective because it does not require the application of judgment to determine whether it has been satisfied; only examination of the literature. Deposition questions that examine whether this criterion has been satisfied are rather easy to create, but the exercise is useful:

   a. *Where has this methodology been published?*

   b. *Who published it?*

   c. *What is the process for pre-publication review?*

   d. *What are the credentials of the reviewers (sometimes called "referees")?*

 e. *What criticisms or suggestions did the reviewers make?*

 f. *What changes were made as a result of those suggestions?*

 g. *What other changes were made?*

 h. *What comments were received post-publication?*

 i. *What is known of the credentials of those persons providing comments?*

 j. *What changes in methodology were made as a result of those comments?*

 k. *Have you, or has anyone else, published additional articles on this methodology?*

2.   Known or Knowable Error Rate

This criterion requests the expert to provide information about the likelihood that the methodology will produce incorrect results. It does not establish a threshold of correctness for admissibility, but it is difficult to believe that a court would admit an expert's opinions after hearing in limine testimony that a methodology may produce wrong results half the time. In the world of commercial litigation, economists and financial analysts may be the experts most susceptible to challenge based on a failure to satisfy this criterion; in truth, are they able even to assess their error rates when they conclude that a particular market structure is more competitive than another?

a. *Identify studies that have calculated error rates for this methodology.*

b. *Describe how you yourself would determine the error rate.*

c. *What mechanisms are available for reducing or eliminating errors?*

d. *Is there a particular aspect of the methodology (e.g., data collection, data input, interpretation of results) that is more likely to produce errors?*

e. *How would someone employing this methodology know that an error had occurred?*

f. *What types of errors can occur?*

g. *What effect would those errors have on the utility or correctness of your opinion?*

Deposition Rules

3. General Acceptance in the Relevant Scientific Community

This is the (previously) well-established *Frye*[6] test. The weakness of this test was not that it asked an irrelevant question—the question is indeed relevant—but rather that it depended upon the expert for an opinion on the reliability of the methodology, rather than seeking objective information. As a sole criterion, however, it also assumes that the court could identify the relevant scientific community. Today, with specialists within specialties within sub-areas within practice areas within medical board areas, as an example, the nests of Russian dolls prevent any court from knowing, on its own, whether this is a "relevant scientific community" or sub-specialty that should be evaluated according to standards from a larger group, or merely a fringe group of radicals. Furthermore, while mechanical engineering methodology may quite reasonably be scrutinized by application of the standards of mechanical engineering, as it was in *Kumho Tire*, we are not so confident that aromatherapist methodology should be evaluated only by application of the standards of

---

6. *See* Frye v. United States, 293 F. 1013 (D.C. Cir. 1923).

aromatherapists. There is a skepticism here that we recognize and believe to be appropriate, even while we understand that we must be able to distinguish it from mere bias or prejudice.

What evidence is there that practitioners in your field generally accept this approach?

   a. How do you define your field?

   b. What other approaches are utilized in that field?

   c. What approach is utilized most often?

   d. What are the advantages and disadvantages of the main methodologies?

   e. Why did you choose to use this methodology?

   f. When was this methodology developed?

   g. What effect did introduction of this methodology have on the acceptance of other methodologies?

4.   Testability or Replicability

It is not sufficient for a researcher to state that she has discovered a relationship between certain effects and a purported cause. She must specify that relationship in a sufficiently specific way that other researchers can examine it for themselves. If their examinations corroborate her results, then the hypothesis may become accepted. Without such corroboration, however, her hypothesis stands as no better than conjecture. For example, several years ago at the National Heart, Lung and Blood Institute, a researcher noted a statistically significant correlation between people who ate sandwiches for lunch and people who developed serious heart disease. The researcher spelled out his methodology in sufficient detail that other researchers could review his approaches and data; they discovered that sandwiches and heart disease were not directly related to each other, but each was instead related to hurried meal times, a characteristic of Type A personalities at high risk for heart disease because of multiple stress factors. The original researcher's problem of *multicolinearity* would not have been observed if the original hypothesis had not been stated with sufficient specificity to permit test and replication.

> a. *Step by step, how have you conducted your tests or examinations?*

b. *Identify all of your data sources.*

c. *Provide all of your laboratory or session notes.*

d. *Beginning with a particular item of raw (empirical) data, show us how it is treated or manipulated by the methodology.*

e. *What tests did you do yourself to confirm that the methodology produced parallel results for parallel inputs? (If your methodology is addition and you input [2, 2] and get 4, then when you input [4, 4] you should get 8.)*

f. *What tests did you do to confirm that disparate inputs would yield disparate results? (If the factor of few firms in an industry is said to lead to high profits, then we should not observe industries with many firms also enjoying high profits. For a simpler analogy, if a friend says that a black box will light a red light when salted pretzels are inserted, it is not a sufficient test to insert salted pretzels and watch for the light; we must also insert unsalted pretzels and stale Gummi Bear candies and watch for the light. Otherwise, we might merely have a machine (methodology) that turns on a light when anything is inserted.)*

5. Development and Use of the Methodology in Nonlitigation Contexts

The Ninth Circuit, on remand in the *Daubert* matter, grafted an additional criterion onto the four suggested by the Supreme Court: Was the methodology developed for nonlitigation purposes?[7] Questioning on this criterion should be reasonably straightforward, because it asks the expert for historical facts, not scientific opinions or relationships. If the methodology was developed solely (or, logically, primarily) for the purpose of supporting a particular side in litigation, we are more skeptical about its objectivity.

    a. When was this methodology developed?

    b. Who was the developer?

    c. What was the original purpose of its development?

    d. Are you using any modifications that were developed for litigation?

---

7. *See* Daubert v. Merrell Dow Pharmaceuticals, Inc., 43 F.3d 1311 (9th Cir. 1995).

e. *Why were modifications made to the original methodology?*

f. *Is the methodology still being used for its original purpose?*

g. *Has it been partially or largely supplanted?*

h. *What methodologies have supplanted it? Why?*

6. Sufficiency to Explain the Salient Facts

The Supreme Court in *Kumho Tire* expressed skepticism that a practitioner of a legitimate methodology ("visual and tactile tire failure analysis") could not evaluate whether an apparently salient fact was present (whether the tire had traveled 50,000 miles or more).[8] This does involve the a priori belief on the part of the Court that this factor is significant; nevertheless, the expert should at least have been able to provide a reasonable explanation for his inability to determine this fact.

---

8. *See Kumho Tire*, 526 U.S. at 254.

   a. *Describe all of the categories of information that were available to you for this analysis (or that are generated by the event being analyzed: profits, margins, gross sales revenue, industry concentration, firm rank, unit sales, advertising-to-sales ratios, advertising expenditure ramps, etc.).*

   b. *Rank those categories of data from most to least significant and explain the ranking.*

   c. *Show us where each of those categories was used.*

   d. *Tell us why some categories of data were not used.*

   e. *Tell us how you adjusted for your inability to obtain some data (e.g., tire travel miles).*

   f. *Have you considered different data in other cases? Why?*

   g. *Do other researchers consider other data or rank the data differently in importance?*

   h. *Have you ever reached conclusions without data from each category?*

7. Quantitative Sufficiency of the Data Employed

In an industrial conveyor belt failure case,[9] the court was concerned that the mechanical engineer was relying on a very small sample to provide data points for his analysis: a few bolts from a very large conveyor assembly. While testimony from someone trained in statistical methods might satisfy the court that the data were sufficient for conclusions at a reasonable level of certainty, the mechanical engineer could not provide that foundation, and the court was uncomfortable with the minimal basis.

   a. *What were your sources of data?*

   b. *How much data was available from each source?*

   c. *Was there richer data available elsewhere?*

   d. *Was a statistical analysis performed to determine the adequacy of the data for the purpose of drawing conclusions?*

---

9.   Watkins v. Telsmith, 121 F.3d 984 (5th Cir. 1997).

    e. At what confidence level did the data allow you to draw your conclusions?

    f. At what confidence level do you typically operate in nonlitigation activities in your profession?

    g. In your last published article, what confidence level did you employ?

    h. In the last article that you read or refereed, what confidence level was employed?

    i. If the data points were increased by a factor of two, how would the confidence level have been affected? If the points were increased tenfold?

    j. If one-third of the data you used were determined to be unreliable, would your conclusions still be sound, at the same level of confidence?

8. Qualitative Sufficiency of the Data Employed

In some cases, we can imagine that the data are quantitatively sufficient (we have enough data points to satisfy the statisticians among us), but we are troubled by the quality of the data or its sources. For example, in child abuse cases, experts sometimes are willing to testify based in part on their experiences with descriptions of abuse and its sequela from numerous children. The sample may be sufficient in size; even the simple hearsay nature of the bases may be so commonly encountered that it does not disqualify the testimony; but the impressionable nature of the sources—children interviewed under unknown and perhaps uncontrolled circumstances, having been subjected to unrevealed pressures or influences—renders them suspect and may impel a court to exclude the expert testimony.

a. What were the sources of your data?

b. Who collected the data?

c. Who supplied the data to the persons collecting it?

d. What prior experience have you had with this methodology for data collection?

e. What tests did you conduct to determine that your data were accurate?

> *f. What motivations were provided to the sources to encourage accurate reporting?*
>
> *g. Were there any penalties for inaccurate reporting by the sources to your collectors?*
>
> *h. What were the sources told about the purposes of the data collection?*
>
> *i. What were the collectors told about the purposes?*
>
> *j. What were the criteria for including and excluding sources of data?*

9. Consistency with General Methodology

Methodologies should be reliable regardless of the context-based biases or prejudices of the persons employing them. For example, the methodology the expert uses to determine the quality of structural steel should be the same, whether that examination is being done as quality control for an industry member, as consultant to a plaintiff in a contract suit, or as consultant to a defendant in a products liability suit. Of course, the general approach should be identified first at deposition, before questioning about specifics; otherwise, the description of what is generally done will be adjusted to match what the witness already said was done in this case. In *Kumho Tire* itself, the Court was interested in the fact that the expert said that his approach involved analysis of four "visual and tactile" aspects of the failed tire and, if any two were present, concluding that the failure was the result of owner abuse rather than manufacturing defect. The expert then found two factors to be present (apparently one just a little bit), but he nevertheless concluded that the failure resulted from defect. This departure from his general methodology may have been fatal to his opinion.[10]

   a. *Tell me the steps in using this analysis in your everyday, nonlitigation work.*

   b. *What are the uses of such analysis?*

   c. *What data do you obtain? From what sources?*

   d. *Who assists you? Why? How?*

---

10. *See Kumho Tire*, 526 U.S. at 254-55.

    e. *When have you used this analysis before?*

    f. *Did you follow the general methodology you have just described?*

    g. *In this litigation, what steps do you perform in this analysis?*

    h. *Who assisted you? Why? How?*

    i. *Was it necessary to depart from the general approach in any way? Why?*

    j. *What precautions did you take to insure that those departures would not inappropriately affect the results of the analysis?*

    k. *What authority did you have for believing those precautions were sufficient?*

    l. *What other steps did you take that were different from your general approach or methodology?*

10. Existence of a Body of Literature on the Particular Methodology

If there is no body of literature on the methodology that the expert is recommending and the explanation for such absence is not apparent or the expert cannot or does not explain the absence of such literature, then the court is justified in exercising skepticism about the reliability of the methodology. (Of course, other factors would be affected also, such as "general acceptance in the relevant scientific community"; how would such acceptance be evidenced if there is no literature?) Of course, if the field of expertise would not be expected to generate such a body of literature ("the adequacy of methods for cleaning tomato sauce spills in supermarket aisles"), the court might well ignore this factor. A faulty syllogism could lead people to believe that because there is a body of literature on an approach, it represents a reliable methodology; it may merely mean that there are lots of unreliable adherents who write lots of unreliable stuff.[11] The field of astrology, as

---

11. In order to be certain that we can identify faulty syllogisms, let us look at a correct syllogism and a faulty syllogism:

- Correct syllogism A: (1) All frogs are green; (2) Clyde is a frog; therefore (3) Clyde is green.

- Correct syllogism B: (1) All frogs are green; (2) Clyde is not green; therefore (3) Clyde is not a frog.

an example, has generated thousands of books and articles over centuries (or millennia, if Druidic runes qualify).

    a. How does one learn about this methodology?

- Incorrect syllogism C: (1) All frogs are green; (2) Clyde is green; therefore (3) Clyde is a frog.

This is incorrect because Clyde could be something else that is green but not a frog, such as a pet lime. Now, applying this syllogistic template to the *Daubert* methodology questions:

- Correct syllogism D: (1) Reliable methodologies are likely to generate relatively substantial literature; (2) this is a reliable methodology; therefore (3) it is likely to generate (or to have generated) a relatively substantial body of literature.

- Correct syllogism E: (1) Reliable methodologies are likely to generate relatively substantial literature; (2) this methodology has not generated relatively substantial literature; therefore (3) this is not a reliable methodology (or, even more correctly, this is not likely to be a reliable methodology).

- Incorrect syllogism F: (l) Reliable methodologies are likely to generate relatively substantial literature; (2) this methodology has generated a relatively substantial body of literature; (3) therefore this is a reliable methodology.

b. *How do you keep up with changes and improvements in the methodology?*

c. *What are the principal journals or publications in this field?*

d. *Who contributes to them?*

e. *Who referees or edits them for methodological correctness?*

f. *Do noted scientists contribute or subscribe? (e.g., do astronomers subscribe or contribute to the "Astrologers' Journal"?)*

g. *Do contributors or editors appear in journals of related and accepted fields? (e.g., do astrologers get published in the "American Journal of Astronomy"?)*

h. *How long have the main journals in the field been published?*

11. Logical Derivation of the Methodology

Experience suggests that the scientific progress is, indeed, progressive; that is, new developments build in some recognizable and articulable way on past, related explorations: blood-letting did not lead immediately to heart transplantations; green Post-It™ notes followed yellow Post-It™ notes; and the methods for putting a human on the moon depended on the development of methods for putting a human in Earth orbit. As a general, a priori principle that makes us comfortable, few steps are skipped. When steps are skipped in such normally evolutionary change, so that it becomes revolutionary, we look for explanations, and we expect the proponent of the new theory to provide those explanations.

   a. Describe the derivation of the methodology that you used.

   b. What prior methodology is this one most closely related to?

   c. Describe the similarities between them. Describe the differences.

   d. What problems or factors led to the change from the old to the new methodology?

   e. Who were the foremost proponents of the prior methodology?

f. *Who initiated, sponsored, or championed the change to the new methodology?*

g. *What role did you have in this change?*

h. *In what circumstances would the two methodologies yield different results?*

i. *What specific differences in the methodologies lead to those different results?*

j. *Why is the new methodology superior?*

Conclusion

The Supreme Court in *Kumho Tire* emphasized that it would be fruitless to attempt to list all criteria for assessing reliability of experts' methodologies because they are as numerous as the fields of human knowledge.[12] The purpose of this article is obviously not to disagree with the Court on this point, but rather to suggest ways of thinking about reliability, approaches to assessing methodologies, that can be used across fields of expertise and that do not depend on requiring the lawyers or the judges to develop competence in

---

12. *See Kumho Tire*, 526 U.S. at 251.

the field being assessed. As we consider these legal questions (both the question of how to determine reliability and the questions being suggested here as part of a solution), we are in fact considering questions of much broader application to the human condition: How do we learn? How do we know when we know? How can we learn what someone else *actually* knows? If we were concerned only with the question—trivial in this context—of determining the credibility of an expert, traditional tools are available: cross-examination, impeachment, learned treatises, omissions, and so forth. Instead, in considering *Daubert-Kumho Tire* issues, we must concern ourselves with the possibility of truth-telling witnesses, armed with patently impressive credentials, whose science may represent the future, but whose testimony should not be presented in court.

CHAPTER EIGHT

VIDEO DEPOSITIONS

8.1 Why Should You Take a Video Deposition?

Video depositions are authorized under Federal Rule of Civil Procedure 30(b)(3)(A). They are useful to capture the witness's demeanor, which can be shown to the trier of fact. They are also much more interesting than transcribed testimony read in court. Where a deposition witness uses visual materials (especially at a deposition taken in anticipation of the unavailability of the deponent for trial), a video deposition may be the only effective way of proceeding that allows the eventual audience—the trier of fact—to enjoy the help of the illustrative and other visual exhibits.

Video recording a deposition may also be an effective—perhaps the only effective—way to control obstreperous counsel. With the camera angle set wide enough to capture the witness and both counsel, the mere presence of a visual record may itself prevent defending counsel from cueing the witness with speaking objections, hand signals, or nods, and it may also prevent questioning counsel from attempting to annoy, embarrass, or oppress the deponent, or otherwise gain an unfair advantage. Even if disruptive counsel cannot be captured on video, the tone of the objections and comments will be available to play for the magistrate or judge, if necessary.

Practice Comment

The scene shown by the video must obviously include the deponent, but many of the video depositions produced today present the witness against an unflattering background with a foreground that looks like the interrogation table at a penitentiary. Deposing counsel might want defending counsel in the picture also, to prevent improper behavior; in fairness, then, both counsel should be visible. Because you can anticipate reluctance on the part of defending counsel to be included, you should seek a protective order in advance, directing defending counsel (or both counsel) to appear on the video. A basis for this order would be prior obstreperous conduct by counsel. Before seeking such an order, attempt to reach agreement on such an approach. If you cannot obtain such an agreement, however, a motion for a protective order under Rule 26(c)(1) is appropriate.

8.2 How Do You Adjust Your Defense in a Video Deposition?

An additional element must be added to counsel's preparation when the opponent notices a video deposition of her witness. Previously, counsel cared about how the deponent came across in a black-and-white, typewritten transcript. Now she must be concerned with how the witness looks. Explicitly discuss with the deponent what he intends to wear to the deposition; while the deponent's clothing should still be comfortable, it must also show the eventual viewers that the witness understood the seriousness of the occasion. For business people and experts, "Friday" or "business casual" attire is out; "important client meeting" attire is in. For blue-collar workers, cleaned and pressed work clothing is fine. For home office workers, they should go back to the attire they used to wear when they met with clients downtown.

Furthermore, counsel must pay attention to the surroundings in which the witness will be displayed. As mentioned previously, the scene shown by the video must obviously include the deponent, but many of the video-recorded depositions produced today present the witness against an unflattering background of institutional green paint, with a foreground that looks like the interrogation table at some police precinct. When the defending lawyer receives a notice for video deposition, she will gain an advantage if she can host the deposition at her offices. She can then arrange the scene for the witness, placing the witness in a room with pleasant-colored walls, perhaps a credenza in the background, with a nice (not too detailed) painting on the wall. A blotter and some other office tools on the desk will reduce the look of an interrogation and make it look more like an interview.

During the video deposition, counsel needs to refrain from talking with the witness while the camera is running. Instead, where she needs to communicate with her witness, she should take a break and take the witness and the discussion outside the room. Deposing counsel may complain, but there is no way that he can keep the lawyer and witness in the room, short of having a court order.

8.3 How Do You Obtain Rulings on Objections to Material in a Video Deposition?

Where the deposition was taken by video recording or sound recording, material submitted to the court for ruling on objections must be presented in the form of a written transcript (FED. R. CIV. P. 32(c)). This provision makes it easier for the court to review challenged material from a non-stenographically recorded deposition. The parties designate the portions of the depositions they intend to use, and the court can then (or at trial) review objections that were made at the deposition or were automatically preserved, like relevance. The parties then prepare an edited video.

8.4 When Do You Need a Paper or Computer Transcript of a Video Deposition?

As noted immediately above, objections arising in a video or audio deposition must be submitted to the court for rulings in the form of a written transcript. If you intend to use the deposition at trial for some purpose other than impeachment (because, in theory, you did not know that the impeachment would be necessary), you must provide a transcript to the other parties in advance of trial (FED. R. CIV. P. 26(a)(3)(B)). In a jury trial, on the other hand, where you intend to use a transcript of what was taken at a video or audio deposition, any other party may require that you present it in the form in which it was taken, unless the court rules otherwise (FED. R. CIV. P. 32(c)).

8.5 How Do You Use a Video Deposition at Trial?

At trial, when a video or audio recording is to be used for impeachment purposes, the evidentiary foundation is identical to that of a written transcript. The witness should be asked virtually the same question posed in the deposition (or asked a question that is actually her deposition answer, changed in format into a question); when she answers "no" instead of "yes," or "green" instead of "blue," you should go into the traditional setup (assuming that this is first time that this witness has been impeached with the deposition).

Q: The light was green for the east-bound Cadillac, wasn't it?

A: No, the Caddy had the red light.

Q: You remember coming to my office two months ago for your deposition?

Q: Your counsel, Mr. Shadis, came with you?

Q: We met in a comfortable conference room?

Q: Your lawyer sat right next to you?

Q: We had beverages and donuts available?

Q: We took breaks when you asked for them?

Q: You were placed under oath by a court reporter?

Q: You knew that the court reporter would write down my questions and your answers?

Q: There was also a cameraman there, with a video camera?

Q: You knew that the video cameraman would record my questions and your answers?

Q: And I asked you this question, and you gave this answer, didn't you? Counsel, this appears at time 33:71:15 of the video. Mr. Osmond [*paralegal*], would you please play that portion?

> "Question: What color was the light for the Cadillac, going east?"

> "Answer: The Caddy? The Caddy
> had a green light."

Q: That was your answer, wasn't it, Mr.
Barker?

Subsequent impeachments of the same witness
with the deposition can omit all of the questions
up to the confrontation of the witness with the
answer from the video; those preliminary questions
are intended to let the jury know that the deposition was not an unfair, star-chamber proceeding.

Where the deposition, video or otherwise, is
offered for purposes other than impeachment,
such as an opposing party's statement or testimony
of an absent witness, the attorney should inform
the court of the foundational facts:

> Your Honor, opposing counsel has
> stipulated that John Larson is the vice
> president of sales of the Landsforth
> company, the opposing party here. We
> offer two minutes of the video of the
> Larson deposition, which is relevant
> to show knowledge of the information
> exchange among competitors. We have

a written transcript of those pages for you, which we designated pretrial. With the court's permission, we would like to play that portion of the video deposition.

8.6 When Should You Use the Video Deposition at Trial?

Video depositions are useful when counsel's good witness is unavailable (and she has taken a preservation deposition or fortuitously created a persuasive video narrative when her opponent took her witness's deposition). Video depositions can also be very effective for impeachment, although this process should not be used too often with a single witness, because it is cumbersome and time consuming to go back and forth from live to video. Anticipate your needs and select a few significant areas for impeachment and limit yourself to those. Video depositions of experts describing their methodology or using demonstrations and illustrative exhibits can win the day when used to resist motions under *Daubert* to preclude or limit expert testimony, especially if the expert is showing something that the court believes it would be interested in seeing during the trial. In opening statements, video clips from the depositions of the officers and agents of the opposing party may effectively take away defenses or rebuttal before the other side has even mentioned the issues. Counsel should be careful not to use *all* the video clips on the point; she wants her actual proof to exceed her promises.

CHAPTER NINE

SEVEN WAYS TO USE DEPOSITIONS AT TRIAL

9.1 Testimony of an Absent Witness.

Where witnesses have become unavailable for trial, either because they are beyond the reach of the court's process or are physically or mentally unfit to attend and give testimony, their deposition testimony may be used in place of their live testimony. Witnesses who have no recollection of the events (but knew at one time) are considered to be "unavailable" under this rule (FED. R. EVID. 804(a)). In court, counsel offers proof or a stipulation that the witness is unavailable through no fault of his client, and then he directs the court's attention to the *short* portion of the deposition he would like to read or play and asks the court for permission to proceed. Proof of unavailability due to failed memory could be had by the witness on the stand asserting that he does not remember.

The opposing party may ask that counsel who is offering the original portion be required to introduce additional portions that, in fairness, the trier of fact ought to consider at the same time (because they clarify or provide context, for example) (FED. R. CIV. P. 32(a)(6); FED. R. EVID. 106). The court often tells opposing counsel that he can introduce such portions in his own examination, an unsound approach because it completely destroys the purpose of the rules of fairness and completeness, which work to keep related extrinsic testimony together in the jury's mind. Nevertheless, the approach does keep opposing counsel from interrupting the presentation and rhythm of counsel who is questioning the witness.

9.2 Past Recollection Recorded.

Under Federal Rule of Evidence 803(5), a deposition may constitute "past recorded recollection," and therefore, if relevant, portions may be read into the record without violating the rule excluding hearsay. However, since counsel must first attempt to refresh and then establish that the witness no longer remembers, it is just as easy to proceed with this forgetful witness by treating him as an "absent" witness, as discussed in the immediate preceding paragraph. (*See* the discussion, in the "absent witness" section above, about handling additional portions of the transcript requested by opposing counsel.)

9.3 Basis for Proffer.

Occasionally, perhaps In reaction to a relevance or foundation objection, the court wants to know why questioning counsel believes, in good faith, that a question will obtain admissible evidence (that is, evidence that is relevant and useful and does not violate Rule 403). By showing the court the actual answers in a deposition, counsel establishes his good faith and lets the court See that the information sought is proper. This is a *proffer*.

9.4 Refreshing Recollection.

Since *anything* can be used to refresh recollection (the question being not what refreshed the recollection, but rather has the recollection truly been refreshed), a deposition (of this or another witness) may be used to bring the memory back to life. The evidentiary foundation is established by:

- asking whether the witness remembers the fact (the color of the light);

- when he says he does not remember, showing the particular section of the deposition (without disclosing its contents to the jury, but advising opposing counsel where the section is located in the transcript);

- taking away the transcript (to emphasize that any answer comes from refreshed recollection, not mere reading);

- asking whether his recollection or memory has been refreshed ("yes, it has"); and

- asking the question again.

9.5 Source of Opposing Party Statement (or Admission).

Under Rule 801(d)(2)(A), opposing party statements are not barred by the rule excluding hearsay; indeed, in the federal system, they are defined as not being hearsay at all, while in some states they are dealt with as the first exception to the rule excluding hearsay. Therefore, party statements need merely be relevant to be admissible (assuming that there is no problem with authenticating them as statements actually made by the party; there is no privilege problem since presumably people outside any privilege now have heard the statement). So all of the relevant statements that you like that were made by the opposing party in a deposition can be admitted at trial, whether that party is on the stand or not. You determine at what point to introduce the statement in your case; you ask the court for permission to read a *short* portion of the opposing party's deposition as an opposing party's statement relevant to the question of whether there was a contract, or the horse escaped, or the fire did more good than harm. (*See* the discussion in the "absent witness" section above of the handling of additional portions of the transcript requested by opposing counsel under Federal Rule of Civil Procedure 32(a)(6) and Federal Rule of Evidence 106.)

9.6 Impeachment.

A full-blown impeachment, and instructions for conducting it, is shown in section 8.5, above.

9.7 Phantom Impeachment.

Here is the circumstance: the deposition transcript has nice red covers, and the witness's name appears in two-inch block letters on the cover. While you listen to direct, you also refer to the deposition volume and insert yellow sticky notes in it. Once cross-examination begins, you use the deposition a number of times to impeach the witness, each time to good effect. Everyone sees the witness cringe each time you reach for the transcript. Now you have reached a point where you and the witness both know what the truth is-the car was red-but you know that fact is not in the transcript. The witness is not certain whether it is in the transcript or not. You ask, "The car was red, wasn't it?" as you reach for the deposition volume. The witness hesitates; the red covers open; the witness watches counsel select a yellow tab; the witness, fearing another painful impeachment, says, "Yes, the car was red."

You could not have impeached the witness with the transcript, and you knew it. But the witness didn't. Some think this is improper, that counsel is misleading the witness. But suggesting that counsel knows and can prove the truth if the witness lies again is really not misleading in any objectionable way. ("Objection, your Honor; he is suggesting that the witness should tell the truth"?) This is phantom impeachment.